COME TO THE
GARDEN

COME TO THE GARDEN

A SWING FOR TWO AWAITS YOU

DAN LUEHRS

TATE PUBLISHING
AND ENTERPRISES, LLC

Published by Tate Publishing & Enterprises, LLC
127 E. Trade Center Terrace | Mustang, Oklahoma 73064 USA
1.888.361.9473 | www.tatepublishing.com

Tate Publishing is committed to excellence in the publishing industry. The company reflects the philosophy established by the founders, based on Psalm 68:11,

"The Lord gave the word and great was the company of those who published it."

Book design copyright © 2017 by Tate Publishing, LLC. All rights reserved.
Cover design by Norlan Balazo
Interior design by Jimmy Achapero Jr.

Published in the United States of America

ISBN: 978-1-68429-445-9
Religion / Christian Life / Spiritual Growth
16.11.09

COME TO THE GARDEN

Gardens are wonderful places; millions of people frequently visit public gardens and parks throughout the world. Just the name alone conjures up feelings of warmth, welcome, and peace. In fact, I have never heard of anyone not liking a garden of some type. Near where I live in Florida, we have gardens called Busch Gardens, Bok Gardens, Sunken Gardens, Botanical Gardens, Cypress Gardens, and our own home we call, Destiny Lane Garden. To be in a flower garden is to be surrounded by the natural beauty and life that invites people to come and adore its ever-changing decor. There are not two gardens alike in the world because there has never been two people alike that have created one. What one person considers being lovely, another would like to see something totally different in the same place. But no matter what one's taste is, gardens take much time and work to plant and cultivate, and I guess that's why so few people have gardens at their homes. We are just too busy with the things of life to take care of one and enjoy it.

> And the Lord God planted a garden toward the east, in Eden; and there He placed the man whom He had formed. (Gen. 2:8, NASB)

God also likes gardens. In fact, it was He who created the first garden in Eden that He had placed man into for his good pleasure. *Eden* means "delightful or pleasure," and I guess that's what gardens are—delightful! God Himself enjoyed this garden so much that He walked through it with the man that He had created it for: "And they heard the sound of the LORD God walking in the garden in the cool of the day" (Gen. 3:8, NASB).

One of Jesus's favorite places was the garden of Gethsemane. The place was so well known to His disciples that Judas knew exactly where to find Jesus on the night that he betrayed Him.

> When Jesus had spoken these words, He went forth with His disciples over the ravine of the Kidron, *where there was a garden, into which He Himself entered*, and His disciples. Now Judas also, who was betraying Him, knew the place; for *Jesus had often met there* with His disciples. (John 18:1–2, NASB, emphasis mine)

It is interesting to note that Jesus had to cross the brook Kidron. *Kidron* means "a dark and gloomy place" that He had to cross to get to Gethsemane. *Gethsemane* means "oil press." This was the place where the pressure on Jesus was so overwhelming that He sweated, as it were, great drops of blood. We also will have to go through some dark and trying situations for us to enter our own Gethsemane, our place of great pressure and dying to self as I have learned in my own life experiences.

Preston Eby wrote the following regarding the garden:

> Now in the place where He [Jesus] was crucified there
> was a *garden*; and in the garden a new tomb wherein
> was never man yet laid. There then because of the Jew's
> preparation [for the tomb was nigh at hand] they laid
> Jesus. (John 19:41–42, KJV)

Of this "garden tomb," we further read,

> When even was come, there came rich man from
> Arimathaea, named Joseph, who also himself was Jesus'
> disciple; this man when to Pilate, and asked for the body
> of Jesus. Then Pilate commanded it to be given up. And
> Joseph took the body, and wrapped it in a clean linen
> cloth, and laid it in his own new tomb, which he had
> hewn out the rock; and he rolled a great stone to the door
> of the tomb, and departed. (Matt. 27:57–60, KJV)

We find by the Word of God that in the place where Jesus
was crucified, there was a *garden* belonging to a rich man
named Joseph. That this garden was carefully tended is implied
by Mary Magdalene mistaking Jesus for the gardener. In this
garden, according to a custom of those days, Joseph had hewn
out for himself a tomb in the rock, and in this tomb, upon a
bed of spices most fragrant and costly, Joseph laid the body of
our precious Lord. Let all men take note that it was in a *garden*,
overshadowed by darkness that covered the whole land, amid
the quaking of the earth and the rending of the rocks, which
Jesus Christ, the second Adam, died. It was amid the opening
of tombs, from which rose many of the saints who had fallen
asleep, that He *rose from the dead*! And I can declare to you that

when He arose on that glad morning, He brought up with Him out of spiritual death all who believe on His Name throughout all ages, and He gave unto them eternal life. *Death came through the first Adam in the Garden of Eden, and eternal life came through the second Adam in the Garden of the Cross and of the Tomb.*

In order to open the way into the greater Garden of the Lord or the Kingdom of Heaven, our Lord went through two gardens. The first was the Garden of Gethsemane, in which He rose concerning the last garden, which is the Garden of the Cross and the Tomb. In the last, He finished the work, which would open the Kingdom of Heaven to all who would believe in His Name. It was in the Garden of Gethsemane that He chose that the will of the Father should be done and naught else.

> Man began in a garden. He sinned in a garden. He died in a garden. He was driven forth from the Garden. Jesus came. He passed through two gardens. He opened up the third garden. *The third Garden is the first Garden. As the first Adam died in the Garden* (of Eden), so the last Adam entered into death in the Garden (of the Cross and Tomb). *The first Adam brought forth death out of life in the Garden while the last Adam brought forth life out of death in the Garden.*

Even though God created the garden of Eden perfectly in the beginning, Adam still needed to cultivate and protect it from intruders: "Then the LORD God took the man and put him into the garden of Eden *to cultivate it and keep* [guard] *it*" (Gen. 2:15, NASB, emphasis mine). God knew there was going to be trouble in paradise and that the enemy of our souls wanted to destroy this new place of fellowship between God and man. Yet the saddest news in the whole Bible is that God had to drive man out of this place of fellowship with his God because man did not guard it as he was told to. "So he drove out the man; and he placed at the east of the garden of Eden Cherubims, and a flaming sword which turned every way, *to keep the way of the tree of life*" (Gen. 3:24, KJV, emphasis mine). Man now was turned away from the path to the tree of life that he once was on. He is now enslaved to sin and death, and only through the cross of Jesus can he get back on the path of life again.

We must understand that the garden represents man in the presence of the life of God! Man with the incorruptible life of God available to him, even as we today have life through Jesus, the Tree of Life. Since God drove man from the garden of life, it could now only be *God Himself* who opens up the way for man to *enter back into life* to be made a partaker of the divine life! "No man *can come* to Me, except the Fathers which hath sent Me *draw him*" (John 6:44, emphasis mine). Again, "And I, if I be lifted up [on the cross] from the earth, *will draw* all men unto Me" (John 12:32).

You may have said to yourself, "Boy, I wish I could have been in the garden of Eden with God." I have good news for you: you can! God has prepared a private garden just for Him and you!

The Garden of Your Heart

Listen! *I am standing at the door*, knocking; if you hear
my voice *and open the door, I will come in to you and eat
with you*, and you with me.

—Revelation 3:20 (NRSV)

God has now prepared this marvelous garden inside each one
of us so that we might have fellowship with Him at any time or
place! Satan tries to duplicate the garden of God through yoga
or eastern meditation, but he fails greatly! We, as the people
of God, must learn how to open the door of our heart to have
fellowship with Jesus inside of us because now the kingdom of
God and His garden abides inside our heart. The old hymn "I
Come to the Garden" catches the pleasure of us being alone with
God in our garden: "I come to the garden alone, while dew is
still on the roses; and the voice I hear, falling on my ear, the Son
of God discloses. And He walks with me, and talks to me, and
tells me I am His own, and the joy we share as we tarry there,
none other has ever known." Only God and you alone know the
pleasures of this secret place.

In the mid-1980s, I learned of this garden as I was seeking
the Lord, and now I try to enter it daily. Even though I must
admit that I really did not know then what I had found, I knew
I liked it and wanted to spend as much time there as I could! I

began to seek the Lord in the evenings after work for two hours of worship and reading my Bible.

This was strange for me because I was used to being so busy doing many other things that I enjoyed. But once I opened this door, entered the garden, and began fellowshipping with God in spirit, I had to enter again and again. Then He began to teach me His ways. I did not want to do anything else in my extra time but seek Him. It was almost like being in another world, and in fact, it was. It was His world, and all I had to do was open the door of my heart, and He came in to fellowship with me! It was, and *is*, a place of wonder of wonders, as if I had entered a new room. I would say to myself, *What is this place?* Yet all I wanted to do was gaze upon Him and this heavenly realm. It had ruined me from enjoying worldly things.

Even people in my church thought I had gone nuts because I would not play softball or go to weeknight services or be a deacon or teach a Bible study because I felt this was God's will for me, to spend time with Him. I just wanted to be with God and sit in His presence and look upon His glory that I was now seeing so clearly. I didn't fully understand what was happening to me; I only knew that this was a place of peace and joy like none other.

Yet it was a dark and costly place to enter, even as Gethsemane was. It was a place of being humiliated before Christian friends and family members because they did not or could not understand me and would make fun of me and fight against me. "My beloved [Jesus] *has gone down to his garden* [us], *to the beds of balsam*, to pasture his flock in the gardens and gather lilies" (Songs 6:2, NASB, emphasis mine).

Many years later, a friend of mine would call me and say, "I now know what you meant when you told me about being alone with God! It is so wonderful, and I now understand what you were doing *down* in your basement for those many years." I had truly found the garden of the Lord and His "beds of balsam" (fragrant spices). But, oh, the fight to get there! But, oh, the joy that *fills* my soul!

We must open the door of our heart to have fellowship with Jesus. He will not make us seek Him.

> *For the gate* [door] *is small*, and the way is narrow *that leads to life* [the tree of life], and few are those who find it. (Matt. 7:14, NASB, emphasis mine)

> But you, when you pray, *go into your inner room* [your heart], and when you have *shut your door*, pray to your Father who is in secret [being hidden], and your Father who sees in secret will repay you. (Matt. 6:6, NASB)

The only way for this door to be opened is from the inside of us for us to have true fellowship with God in spirit. He will not open the door to His treasury of truths if we are selfishly seeking to promote ourselves in any way. We must take the initiative *to go down* into the garden, which is a place of humility for our flesh and before our family and friends who know what we are dong. "My beloved has *gone down* to his garden." Just think how much He must humble Himself to come into us. Is it too much for Him to ask that we humble ourselves before Him and others? For when we come into His garden, it has a river flowing through it. This waters all those who come and humble themselves to the lowest level because that is where the waters of the Holy Spirit flow freely. This gives us great incentive for us to humble ourselves before Him so that we will never run dry. Water always flows to the lowest level. "And a river went out of Eden to water the garden" (Gen. 2:10, KJV).

David knew and partook of this river that flowed through the garden to quench his thirsty soul with its pure flowing waters. "As the deer pants for the water brooks, so my soul pants for Thee, O God. *My soul thirsts for God, for the living God; when shall I come and appear before God?*" (Ps. 42:1–2, NASB, emphasis mine).

We must do a better job of cultivating the weeds of sin out of our lives and guarding the garden of our heart than Adam did. The enemy of our soul will try to get us to walk in sin so that our fellowship with God is broken. He will fight us on this front of spending time with God more than anything else because he knows that if we are spending time with God, we will be growing in the likeness of Jesus.

Whoever we spend time with, we will become like. The devil will use friends, family, busyness, and many other distractions to keep us from spending time with God. But we must fight against his schemes. A. W. Tozer said, "Whatever keeps me from my Bible is my enemy, however harmless it may appear to be, whatever engages my attention when I should be meditating on God and the things eternal does injury to my soul." Amen!

We are called to walk with God in our garden so that He can teach us His ways. What could be better in life than this?

> *A garden enclosed is my sister, my spouse* [bride]; a spring shut up, a fountain sealed. (Songs 4:12, KJV, emphasis mine)

Wade Taylor speaks of this verse in his book, *The Secret of the Stairs*. I quote,

> The Lord made an arrangement where she became as "a garden inclosed" SS 4:12a. Here, she was separated for a time from material influences and outside activities, unto the Lord Himself. During this time of separation within the garden, all that she had come to know about the Lord will become personalized (made personally real) within her spiritual experience. Then, in His time and place, that which she has become while within the Garden will find its full expression and outworking through her daily life experiences. She is about to experience what the Lord meant when He said, "Buy of Me gold tried in the fire" Rev 3:18b.
>
> This "Garden inclosed" was designed to bring forth the very best from the potential that the Lord had seen to be within her. It was situated in a very beautiful setting. However, it represented a realm of intense "personal dealings," so she hesitated in entering. The Lord knew she would attempt to leave before He could accomplish all He desired within her. He therefore built a high wall around the garden, making it completely enclosed so she would not be able to leave. The Lord is able to keep us where He has placed us.

This high wall also hindered all, except the Lord, from entering. It separated her from the fellowship of her friends, and from those who would attempt to occupy her time. Also, during this set-apart time, her gifts seemingly failed to operate, and her "ministry" was cut off. Now, she was separated from all of the people and things, which she had become accustomed to and dependent upon in her spiritual life. She became as a "Garden inclosed," separated unto the Lord Himself.

The nine plants *(SS 4:13–14)* that are mentioned as being in this Garden are types of the nine-fold fruit of the Spirit. These represent the "quality" of life which is beginning to develop and become manifest within her, during this time of separation. The Garden in bloom speaks of the spiritual maturity now unfolding within her, a beautiful display of righteousness, peace, and joy, as she grows in spiritual understanding and wisdom. During this time of being set apart, there was often a desire within her for expression, or ministry: "If I just get out and share this." But the Lord had made her a "Garden inclosed."

Through being shut in by the Lord for a season, she became more sensitive in her ability to recognize His presence, and was able to respond more promptly to His desire for her fellowship. We were created for His pleasure *(Rev 4:1* 1). There are times when the Lord desires to be personally alone with us, that He might sup with us, and then we with Him (Rev 3:20). This will lead us into the experience of the "fellowship of His sufferings" Phil 3:10b, as He shares His burdens with us.

There are other areas of separation. There are those who are called to a ministry of intercession. Being an intercessor requires much more from us than our times of prayer. It involves our becoming identified with the problem, or need, in order to pray it through. Intercession is born of the Spirit and operates through inner travail. It means getting alone and wrestling with a burden until it is brought to birth through the agony of birth pains. A ministry of intercession is effectual and is worked out in the prayer closet, alone with the Lord. There are those who are called to this hidden ministry of intercession who are not known to man, but known only to the Lord, and have become as a "Garden inclosed" to Him.

There are others who are shut in with the Lord in hidden ministries, who have had a part in bringing to birth many lives. Some of these had a part in the forming of my spiritual life. During times when I was going through some very intense struggles, through the agony of their intercession and prayers, God was able to accomplish something special within me. Without them, I could not be where I am today. There is great responsibility and reward in a hidden ministry of this type. The Lord is looking to and fro across the earth for someone to "stand in the gap;" someone who will stand between the need and the Lord, and then travail until the Lord is able to move upon the situation and accomplish His purpose.

There are those whom the Lord leads into this "Garden inclosed" to remain there. Some of the Lord's choicest saints are separated from the world and enclosed within this Garden, that He might come to them as He wills, to enjoy times of fellowship and communion. The extravagance that the Lord expressed in His creation is evident to us, which we all enjoy as we witness the manifold and multi-colored flowers of spring, and then the rich brilliance of color in the departing leaves of fall. So also, He can afford the luxury of being extravagant in setting aside "whom He will" for His purpose and glory. Thus, within this "Garden inclosed" are those who are so completely given to Him that they are known to Him alone.

There are still others whom the Lord draws into this Garden to stay for only a limited time. He leads these back out again to become a witness of all they received while there alone in the Garden with Him Whom they love. Those who desire more of the Lord, but are not yet ready to be drawn into this Garden experience, will be able to pick fruit from the lives of these who had been within, until they also desire to come within this "Garden inclosed."

When the Lord came into the Garden to be with His Bride-as He had entered the Garden of old "in the cool of the day [evening]" Gen. 3:8, to walk with Adam-she experienced the peace and the joy that results from being in His presence. As she basked in the warmth of this presence, she prayed that the wind (the Holy Spirit) would come and blow upon her Garden. She desired new inward beauty that was developing within her to become as a beautiful fragrance that would flow out from her being, and bless Him.

Jesus wants His garden to produce fruit so that He can eat of it. "Awake, O north wind, and come, wind of the south; *Make my garden breathe out fragrance*, let its spices be wafted abroad. *May my beloved come into his garden and eat its choice fruits!*" (Songs 4:16, NASB, emphasis mine). Notice the wording: "Make my garden breathe out fragrance!" These north winds are the hard and difficult days and years that we all are go through, but He says that this is what causes us to produce good fruit.

So why would we run from these north winds when they are producing such a great work in us? He desires us to grow so that our fragrance would blow in the winds and fill the air with His fragrance of love! "*For we are a fragrance of Christ* to God among those who are being saved and among those who are perishing" (2 Cor. 2:15, NASB, emphasis mine). Oh, the bitterness of these north winds! But take courage, for the south winds will also come with great blessings!

God calls those who have fellowship with Him daily in their hearts *His bride*: "*I have come into my garden, my sister, my bride; I have gathered my myrrh along with my balsam. I have eaten my honeycomb and my honey; I have drunk my wine and my milk. Eat, friends; drink and imbibe deeply, O lovers*" (Songs 5:1, NASB, emphasis mine). He gathers His myrrh, the suffering that we all go through; nothing is wasted with God! But along with the suffering, He gathers our spices so that we are a sweet-smelling aroma unto Him. "But thanks be to God, who always leads us in His triumph in Christ, and *manifests through us the sweet aroma of the knowledge of Him in every place*" (2 Cor. 2:14, NASB, emphasis mine).

He says, "I have eaten my honeycomb and my honey; I have drunk my wine and my milk." Then He says, "Eat, friends; drink and imbibe deeply, O lovers." Again He invites us to eat and dine with Him as He did in Revelation 3:20. But this time, He says, "Imbibe deeply O lovers," or become drunk with My presence and great love! Honey represents His strength that we receive from Him. The wine is the joy that comes to us in His presence for it lifts all darkness. The milk is His sweet word that we are to receive daily to grow strong spiritually.

As I see it now, to walk daily in this garden with Jesus is to walk in heaven, and His Life that surrounds us "for in Him we live, and move, and have our being" (Acts 17:28, KJV). It is a realm or level in the spirit with God that we as Christians must attain to by maturing spiritually. When I say "attain to," I am not talking about working up a prayer life, but learning how to rest and yield to the Spirit of God by being infused with His life and presence, waiting in the Spirit as John the Revelator did in Revelation 1:10: "*I was in the Spirit* on the Lord's day." This is where the treasury of God's truths are all hidden, as John found out. It is in the secret place of our heart that God reveals them to us because all things are hidden in Jesus. Jesus lives in our heart, in spirit, and as we spend time with Him in spirit, He will reveal His secrets to us.

> And I will give you the treasures of darkness, and *hidden wealth of secret places*, in order that you may know that it is I, the Lord, the God of Israel, who calls you by your name. (Isa. 45:3, NASB)

We can live both in the natural and in the spirit realm at the same time, just as Jesus did.

> And no man hath ascended up to heaven, but *he that came down from heaven*, even the Son of man *which is in heaven.* (John 3:13, KJV, emphasis mine)

> And God raised us up with Christ [in spirit] *and seated us with him in the heavenly [spirit] realms* in Christ Jesus. (Eph. 2:6, NIV, emphasis mine)

Yes, believe the truth of God's word. You are already seated with Him in spiritual realms. Now go even higher in Him!

God's promise to us is that He will restore Zion (the church) to the likeness of the garden of Eden again.

> The LORD will surely comfort *Zion* and will look with compassion on all her ruins; *he will make her deserts like Eden, her wastelands like the garden of the* LORD. Joy and gladness will be found in her, thanksgiving and the sound of singing. (Isa. 51:3, NIV, emphasis mine)

> They will say, "*This land that was laid waste has become like the garden of Eden*; the cities that were lying in ruins, desolate and destroyed, are now fortified and inhabited." (Ezek. 36:35, NIV, emphasis mine)

COME INTO THE HIGH PLACES

Now the LORD said to Moses, "*Come up to Me on the mountain* and remain there, and I will give you the stone tablets with the law and the commandment [God's teachings] which *I have written for their instruction.*

—Exodus 24:12 (NASB)

Just what do I mean by the *high places*? There are three plains of life that we can choose to live our lives out on in the earth: (1) the natural sensual realm, which is living to please the body, the lust of the flesh; (2) the soulish realm, which is to be carnally minded, wanting to reason everything out in life according to the ways of the world; and (3) the spirit or heavenly realm where God dwells, which is the *high place* where we are called to sit with Jesus and be taught His ways. This is a realm of righteousness, peace, and joy in the Holy Ghost.

By our daily focusing on the things of God, we can begin to come up into the *high places* with Him. God invited Moses to come up into the mountain or the realm of God (which was a type of spirit realm), and in this heavenly realm, God Himself taught Moses His ways and truths. God alone knew of these teachings that He had Moses write down for us to read. We must understand that it was on the mountain, the "high places," where God taught him. These teaching are now the first five books of the Old Testament, things that no other person had ever heard of or written down before. We can stay on the lower plain of life if we choose to—with fear, worry, depression, and confusion—where the rest of the world lives. Or we can go up into the realm of God.

As Christians, we are to be separate from the ways of the world. Every day we will choose which realm we will be a part of, either God's or the world's! God will not make the choice for us; we must choose daily by our seeking His presence and going after Him and by staying filled with His Spirit. When we seek Him and not the things of the world, we are then going up into the *high places* with the Lord to be taught His ways and truths as Moses was!

> *Come, and let us go up to the mountain of the* LORD, and to the house of the God of Jacob; and *He will teach us* of his ways, and *we will walk in his paths* [the path of life]: for the law shall go forth of Zion, and the word of the LORD from Jerusalem. (Mic. 4:2, KJV, emphasis mine)

Today, it is spiritual Mount Zion that we have been invited to come up into with God, not a natural mountain.

> But *you have come to Mount Zion* and to the city of the living God, *the heavenly Jerusalem,* and to myriads of angels. (Heb. 12:22, NASB, emphasis mine)

For us not to come up into the *high places* of God to be taught His ways will prove to be very foolish on our part! What an opportunity, what a calling we have to be with God in the *high places*!

Since the death and resurrection of Jesus, God has been calling mankind to live on the highest plane of life. However, few have gone up into the *high places* of truth with Him to be changed into His likeness. God meant for man to live in the *high places* with Him in the beginning, but Adam did not obey God and was reduced to being carnal-minded rather than being spiritually minded, which is after the likeness of God. "For those who are according to the flesh set their minds on the things of the flesh, but those who are according to the Spirit, the things of the Spirit" (Rom. 8:5, NASB). Very simply put, if we are focused on the ways of our flesh, we will be worldly minded. If we are focused on God, we will be following after the ways of the Spirit. It all has to do with what we are thinking and focusing on! We must focus upward, not down!

We have been given a wonderful promise in Isaiah 33:16, "*He* [who walks righteously] *will dwell on the heights*; his refuge [safety] will be the impregnable rock [Jesus]; his bread [the Word of truth] will be given him; his water [the filling of the Spirit] will be sure."

What an awesome promise! But first we must walk by the Spirit before we can be taught God's ways (our mind must be renewed daily to His ways). Then we will walk in His paths that He has chosen for us. "He will teach us of His ways, and we will walk in His paths" (Mic. 4:2). The path that He has chosen for me will be different from the path that He has chosen for you; we all have a different calling to fulfill in God's eternal plan of the ages. All I know is, God is a God of the mountains (the good things of life) as well as the God of the valleys in our life (the negative things of life). Israel's enemies found this out when they said, "Thus says the LORD, because the Arameans have said, '*The* LORD *is a god of the mountains, but He is not a god of the valleys;*' therefore I will give all this great multitude into your hand, and you shall know that I am the LORD" (1 Kings 20:28, NASB, emphasis mine). He is the Lord of every area in our life!

The *high places* of God are His truths being revealed in our heart that renew our minds and refresh our spirit. Very few Christians ever seem to choose to venture into these *high places* because of the fear of man and their own insecurities. To climb the *high places* of truth has proved to be much more difficult than what I first thought. I have found it to be a very lonely place at times, with very few people desiring the deeper things of God. But in the natural, there aren't too many people climbing to the mountaintops either!

The Lord spoke to me in 1999 that this would be a lonely place with few people wanting to be with me, as illustrated in the books *Pilgrim's Progress* and *Hinds' Feet on High Places*. This has truly come to pass in my own life. Now I must keep my focus going upward to the *high places* even if none desire to go with me, until the Lord opens the way back to the valley below for me to help others come up and out of the lies and deceptions of the enemy and false religion.

> The LORD God is my strength, and he will make my feet like hinds' feet, and *he will make me to walk upon mine high places.* (Hab. 3:19, KJV, emphasis mine)

The Lord began to reveal to me very clearly that He had prepared me for the *high places* years ago when I began to seek Him daily. He said to me in September of 1998, "I am ready to take you up into the *high places.*" But I did not understand such spiritual language until I read for the third time in 2001 *Hinds' Feet on High Places.* Hannah Hurnard writes:

> Sometimes, as she looked on the glorious panorama visible from these lowest slopes [truths] in the Kingdom of Love, she found herself blushing as she remembered some of the dogmatic statements which she and others had made in the depths of the valley about the High Places and the ranges of Truth [deeper truths]. They had been able to see so little and were so unconscious of what lay beyond and above. If that had been the case down in the valley, how much more clearly, she now realized, that even up on those wonderful slopes [deeper truths] *she was only looking out on a tiny corner of the whole.*
>
> She began to understand quite clearly *that truth cannot be understood from books alone* or by any written words, but *only by personal growth and development in understanding*, and that things written even in the Book of Books can be astonishingly misunderstood while one

still lives on lower levels of spiritual experience (truths) and on the wrong side of the grave on the mountains.

She perceived that no one who finds herself up on the slopes of the Kingdom of Love can possibly dogmatize [be opinionated] about what is seen there, because it is only then that she comprehend how small a part of the glorious whole she sees. All she can do is to grasp with wonder, awe, and thanks giving, and to long with all her heart *to go higher and to see and understand more.*

Lord, that I might receive my sight! Help me to open myself to more light. Help me to fuller understanding.

In August of 1998, the Lord woke me up and said, "I am about ready to reveal My plan to you. Don't quit now, but press on!" Even though at that time I thought it was the plan for ministry, God wanted to give me His plan of the ages, just like He gave Moses on the mountain! *His plan and purpose throughout the ages has been sonship, to have a holy priesthood of believers, a holy nation, who will be the likeness of His Son, so that He could bless and judge the nations through them.*

> Now therefore, if you obey my voice and keep my covenant, you shall be my treasured possession out of all the peoples. Indeed, the whole earth is mine, *but you shall be for me a priestly kingdom and a holy nation.* These are the words that you shall speak to the Israelites. (Exod. 19:5–6, NRSV, emphasis mine)

In May of 2000, Jesus came to me as I was sitting on a dock by the lake; His presence came greatly upon me. For about a week, I had not been able to get into His presence very well, but that night He came powerfully. He came to me and said, "Do you want to go up higher?" I thought, "There is more?" He said, "Yes, My glory!" Then I said, "Yes, I want this." He said, "Follow me!"

After this, a messenger came with a container of water. Then Jesus said, "Cup your hands." As I did, the angel filled them up, and Jesus said, "Now wash your face and eyes and ears." Then the angel filled my hands again, and Jesus said, "Now drink!" I did and said, "What is this?" He said, "My cup." Then I knew what this was about. It meant that I was to suffer to enter the glory as He did.

> Was it not necessary for the Christ to suffer these things
> and to enter into His glory? (Luke 24:26, NASB)

Again in July of 2000, I was preaching in a church in South Dakota, and a lady had a word for me. She took my hand as she was standing on the stage as I stood on the floor, and she said, "The word of the Lord is, 'Come up higher, come up higher, Dan!'" She then pulled me up on stage three different times. She said, "The Lord knows you can't do it on your own, but the Lord will pull you up! It will not happen the way you think it will, but trust the Lord to bring it to pass, for now is the time."

A few days later, another confirming word was mailed to me from a seventy-year-old woman that I did not know. The word was, "God will bring you into a higher realm of experience and revelation because you seek for truth." Even as I received all these confirmations that the Lord was inviting me into the *high places* of truth as He did Moses, I still did not comprehend what it all meant and why I was still suffering so in my finances for this was a great stumbling block for me.

Then in March of 2001, I was in a time of great discouragement, and I received another word from a lady on the phone that I did not know. She prophesied, "I am well pleased with you. I have My hand upon you at this time. You are farther along than you realize. Now is the time when you must spend lots of time with Me that you might 'come up higher' and be changed into My likeness. For it will take many hours in My presence for this to come to pass."

In October of 2001, I had a vision of myself standing on top of a mountain, ready to go back down in the valley to help others up. The song of the waterfalls came to me from *Hinds' Feet on High Places*: "Lower still, lower still we must go!"

How difficult it was for me to understand these wonderful truths of God's word before He invited me into the *high places* because they went against all the tradition that I was taught in the religious church. Certainly they were the *high places* because so few people are willing to climb up and go against the established doctrines of their day because they do not want to be looked down upon in their Christian walk. When God began to reveal His word to me, He had confirmed them in many ways for me to be at peace and receive them fully from Him. The only way I could receive them from Him was for me to *hear His voice and know His presence in them*. God had set up my path so that

I would run into people that had the same message that he had given me. Truly miraculous powers were at work on my behalf! Now that He has given me His plan for the ages, I was told to write the word and wait to see what He would do next. So through faith and patience, I must wait for His next step!

Now that I had written several books about these truths and other books are in the works, I had the revelation that all I was going through must be of God because I could have never done this in my own knowledge and understanding. I was told many years ago in several prophecies that I would do things I didn't know how to do. A great turning point came in my life when I spoke with Rick Joyner about his writings. He said that he had to go over his writings four times and then let others still edit them. This gave me encouragement that I too could write what was in my heart, even though I made so many mistakes. God has given me many great hidden truths that I had asked Him for years ago without knowing that I would write them. He has even given me an editor from Minnesota as God put a burden on Mindy Begnaud's heart to help me edit my books. This was another answer to prayer! Yes, I must continue to write the word of the Lord to fulfill His purpose for my life.

I had received a prophecy on December 31, 1996, that made no sense to me at the time from Jerry Bernard as he was preaching at Carpenter's Home Church in Lakeland, Florida. He stopped by me as he was preaching and said, "You have a lot in you that has not even been tapped yet. God is going to take it out of you, so get ready, it is about to happen. It is your season for the double inheritance to come!" Now I know that this word was from God and that God has placed inside of me His word to write since the foundation of the world. Now it was coming out of me to help bring others into the *high places*. How exciting, but how difficult! Temptations and trials seem to be on every corner to test my faithfulness to the Lord. Even the years prior to these great truths coming to me had been hard, but they were the days of preparation so that I could stand and receive them!

If I had not moved to South Dakota from Minnesota in obedience and then moved to Florida, God could not have entrusted me with these greater truths. I had to pay the price of obedience, both physically and monetarily, in order to receive His truth. Great truth is not given out by God without us having to pay a price for it. Jesus told the church at Laodicea, "I advise you to buy from Me gold [truth] refined by fire [through testings and sufferings], that you may become rich [in truth], and white garments [of holiness], that you may clothe yourself, and that the shame of your nakedness [sin] may not be revealed; and eye salve to anoint your eyes, that you may see [understand spiritual truths]" (Rev. 3:18,a NASB).

Salvation is a free gift to all those who ask, but that does not mean we do not have to pay the price of following our Lord into His greater truths. What happens to many believers is that they stop paying the price of *sacrifice* to go higher into the truths of God. The sacrifice may be to leave a certain job, church, or relocate to wherever the Lord would lead them. The price has always been high to receive great riches, both in the natural and spirit realm.

> *Great truths are dearly bought*, the common truths, such as men give and take from day to day, come in common walk of easy life, blown by the careless wind across our way. *Great truths are greatly won*, not found by chance, nor wafted on the breath of the summer dream; *but grasped in great struggle of soul, hard buffeting with adverse wind and stream. But in the day of conflict, fear and grief, when the strong hand of God, put forth in might, plows up the subsoil of the stagnant heart, and brings the imprisoned truth seed to the light.* Wrung from the troubled spirit, in hard hours of weakness, solitude, perchance of pain, *truth* springs like harvest from the well-plowed field, and the soul feels it has not wept in vain. (Anonymous)

The heavens are now opened to us so that we may go higher into the realm of the spirit than ever before possible, unto the transformation of our mind and body. God is now saying, "*Come up here!*" We must go up and pay the price, not only for our good, but also for the good of mankind. We need to obey the voice of God as He is speaking from heaven. "After these things I looked, and behold, a door standing open in heaven, and the first voice which I had heard, like the sound of a trumpet speaking with me, said, '*Come up here*, and I will show you what must take place after these things'" (Rev. 4:1, NASB, emphasis mine).

When we moved to Florida, God sent me to a little town called Intercession City to minister to a few people for three and a half years. This was very difficult for me; my pride was hurt so badly that I felt as if I was being torn in two! But if I had not obeyed God by staying there, I would not have met Vinnie Bauldree, who gave me Bill Britton's books that taught me so much about the sons of God. This was truly a *high place* in the Spirit of truth for me! The whole journey has been a process of sacrifice and obedience and wondering why God would lead me in such ways. The carnal mind will always be offended at the way the Lord will lead us, and the "higher up" we go in truth, the more trying it becomes because so few people understand the greater truths of the Bible to help us on your journey. In fact, many Christians will fight against us and call us to come back down with them into their church doctrines. And if we don't, they will call us heretics and disassociate from us because they don't understand!

I think God makes it this difficult to see if we will obey Him and cling just to Him, not man! God then can and will entrust us with His hidden treasures of the secret place! "And I will give you the treasures of darkness, and hidden wealth of secret places, in order that you may know that it is I, the LORD, the God of Israel, who calls you by your name" (Isa. 45:3, NASB). When the Lord told me to leave the Assemblies of God as a minister, it boggled my mind. But when I obeyed, it was as if I was let out of the cage of religion to see His greater truths. He then told me to leave the organized church, which was a part of His plan and purpose for my life, so that I could receive more from Him. The greater the sacrifice we have to pay in following the Lord, the greater the reward will be on the other side of that trial! He will then entrust us with His eternal treasures of His word by placing them into our heart and not our head! "Behold, *thou desirest truth in the inward parts*: and in the hidden part thou shalt make me to know wisdom" (Ps. 51:6, KJV, emphasis mine).

Jesus said in Luke 16:11, "If therefore you have not been faithful in the use of unrighteous mammon, who will entrust the true riches [truth] to you?" I have tried my best to be a willing and available vessel for God and to faithfully invest my life and my life savings by moving and giving into what God would have me. Yes, I have made many mistakes in the process, but I have truly been blessed of God and am rich in the treasures of His word and in seeing His faithfulness. But I am willing to give it all away to those who hunger and thirst for truth.

When I look back five years ago to when God told me about the Bible school that He wants to give me, I was still a babe in my scriptural understanding. I cannot imagine what will happen in the next five years and what else He will reveal to me about Himself. But somehow, I believe that all that He has given me is for the purpose of teaching it in the Bible school that He said He would raise up. Oh, how unfathomable are His ways!

Getting High in God

Do not conform any longer to the pattern of this world
[the way the world lives], but be transformed by the
renewing of your mind [by receiving and living the
truth]. Then you will be able to test and approve what
God's will is—his good, pleasing and perfect will.

—Romans 12:2 (NIV)

The enemy has stolen the words "getting high" for long enough. Man has tried on his own to *get high* through the tower of Babel, drugs, alcohol, sex, yoga, and many other false religions to reach a state of euphoria. But these are only poor and temporary substitutes at best and will only prolong that which we seek and desire most—a renewed mind that is full of God's peace and joy continually! Very simply, the *high places* of truth that we are learning will renew our minds *as we learn to live it*, for this is well-pleasing unto the Lord that we are being changed into His likeness for He has promised this in His word. Now is the time for us to *get high* on the revelation of God's truth and get above the world's depression, doubt, fear, and religion! We must not only see Jesus as God or as a person, but as the Truth, the living Word of God that gives us understanding in spiritual realities and sets our mind free from the darkness of false religious and the carnal mind-set!

The mind has a hard time letting go of past indoctrinations because of our insecurities from the fall in the garden. Our mind must be anchored to some ideology, and by us letting go of old ideologies and doctrines, we are humbling ourselves before God and are grabbing something new that we are not quite sure of yet. Change can be quite fearful if we are not secure in our faith and trust in God. But God will help us let go of past doctrines if we are willing to change.

I can remember when I was a Lutheran and got saved. I started going to another church that did not teach infant baptism, but taught a believer's water baptism. At first, hostile thoughts came into my mind against the Bible teacher because he was attacking "my doctrine" that I was taught as a small child and believed wholeheartedly. But when I was shown the scriptures on why we must be baptized after we receive Jesus into our heart, it changed my whole perspective on this one truth. I then went to my family and former pastor with all the Bible verses that I knew on water baptism to tell them this one truth that I received from the Lord. They all concluded that I was in a cult and these people were deceiving and brainwashing me from Lutheranism! For a time, I thought that they might be right, but when I continued to study the word of God and anchor my soul in *His* truth, I was convinced that the word was right and they were the ones deceived by the spirit of religion! Jesus said very clearly to His disciples, "*To you* it has been granted to know the mysteries of the kingdom of heaven, *but to them it has not been granted*" (Matt.

13:11, NASB, emphasis mine). How blessed we are to know and grow in the truth!

I could go on with many other such doctrines that churches say are false doctrines, but in reality are truth. Until we are saved and filled with the Spirit of truth, we will not rightly be able to discern the word of truth. Even after this initial filling, it will take much spiritual growth and understanding in the ways of God and His presence to have a deeper understanding of truth because truth is built in us "line upon line, truth upon truth." The enemy wants to keep us living in the lies of religion so that he can enslave us to man's ways rather than us being free men to go higher into the ways of God and being changed into God's likeness. If the enemy cannot enslave us with religion, he will try to use the sins of the flesh to keep us from going higher. But Jesus said, "And you shall know the truth, and the truth shall make you free" (John 8:32, NASB). Jesus didn't say the truth "might make you free," but that *truth* would set us free from everything! Hallelujah! Learning and believing truth is where the battle is fought the hardest in our mind, but also where the greatest victories are won! Once we have been set free from false doctrines, we are able to use truth to *wisely* set others free from falsehood. How can a person set someone else free that first has not been freed himself? This is why Romans 8:21 is so important to us! "That the creation itself [people] also will be set free *from its slavery* to corruption [sin and death] *into the freedom of the glory of the children of God*" (emphasis mine). There is coming a day when people will want to know the truth that can set them free, and *they will be set free by it*! You can take that to the bank because God has already said it, and that's the end of that!

Climb to the Saving of Soul

> Now may the God of peace Himself sanctify you entirely; and may your *spirit* and *soul* and *body* be preserved complete [completely matured], without blame at the coming of our Lord Jesus Christ.

> —1 Thessalonians 5:23 (NASB), emphasis mine

As believers in these last days, we are awaiting the *revelation* of Jesus Christ (this is His full revealing through His people). This will be our *full salvation, transformation, and deliverance* from sin and death. Then our *spirit, soul,* and *body* will come forth in the exact likeness of Jesus for the entire world to behold and be set free by His glory in us (see Col. 3:4, 1 John 3:2, Rev. 1:7, and Isa. 60:1). Each of us is a triune person; that is, we are a spirit that has a soul (our mind, will, and emotions), and we live in a body. When we received Jesus into our heart, our spirit man came alive through the *seed* of Christ that was implanted within us. This *seed* is the word of God. It is in the exact likeness of Jesus and must grow and mature in us to the *full* likeness of Him!

Even now, our spirit man has the "fullness" of Jesus in it, "for in Christ *all the fullness* of the Deity lives in bodily form, and *you have been given fullness in Christ,* who is the head over every power and authority" (Col. 2:9–10, NIV, emphasis mine). Even though we have already been given the "fullness" of Christ in our inner man, He has not yet manifested Himself through us in such manner because our mind has not been completely renewed into His likeness. This is a process of obedience and of dying to self and takes many years for us to mature and come into His likeness. This why our mind *must be* renewed day by day! "Our inner man is being renewed day by day" (2 Cor. 4:16, NASB).

Our mind will *never* be totally renewed until Jesus *fully* reveals Himself through us in His timing; it will not come about by our striving for it or by our trying to work up enough faith for it to come to pass. It will be a total sovereign work of God. We cannot and will not bring this to pass on our own!

> Listen, I tell you a mystery: We will not all sleep [die],
> but we will all be changed [into Jesus likeness] in a flash,
> in the twinkling of an eye, at the last trumpet. For the
> trumpet will sound, the dead will be raised imperishable,
> and we will be changed. (1 Cor. 15:51–52, NIV)

Even though we cannot bring this to pass in our own power and timing as we would like, we are called to cleanse and purify our mind with the word of truth so that we will be pure, even as He is pure. "Wherefore lay apart all filthiness and superfluity of naughtiness, *and receive with meekness the engrafted* [implanted] *word, which is able to save* [deliver] *your souls* [mind]" (James 1:21, KJV, emphasis mine). It is the word that has the power to purify our mind from the defilement of the flesh and spirit of the world and then prepares us for this great climactic event that we do not want to miss for anything in the world! (See 1 John 3:3, Col. 3:5, and 2 Tim. 2:21.)

> *Who shall ascend into the hill [mountain] of the* LORD*?* Or who shall stand in His holy place? *He that hath clean hands, and a pure heart;* who hath not lifted up his soul unto vanity, nor sworn deceitfully. *He shall receive the blessing from the* LORD, and righteousness from the God of his salvation. *This is the generation of them that seek him, that seek thy face* [that receive the promise]. (Ps. 24:3–6, KJV, emphasis mine)

In 1 Peter 1:5–13, he wrote that *the revelation or the revealing of Jesus* through us is the end of our faith and will be the grace that will bring *full* salvation and *full* deliverance to our soul/mind from the fallen sinful nature that we received through Adam.

"Receiving *the end of your faith, even* the *salvation of* your *souls*" (verse 9, KJV, emphasis mine). The word *your* in this verse is not in the original Greek writing, but was added by the translators and should read, "The salvation of soul!" The revelation of Jesus is what we need and desire most at this time so that the battle between the carnal mind and Spirit of God may be finished within us. Oh, how I long and desire for this to come to pass in me today! But until then, we must fight the good fight of faith and not give up one inch of spiritual ground that we have gained in the renewal of our mind or pull back one bit to the ways of the world or the religious system. We must press on and into God for this to come to pass in us!

The writer of Hebrews said, "But we are not of them who draw back unto perdition [ruin or loss]; but of them that believe [have faith] *to the saving of the soul*" (Heb. 10:39, KJV, emphasis mine). Our perseverance of *faith* is for the purpose of having *our mind saved* or brought back from the fallen nature completely. The word *saving* literally means "the gaining or acquiring salvation in *fullness*." And until our mind is *saved* and *delivered* completely from the power of sin and death, we do not yet possess the *full* salvation that Jesus died to give us.

Hebrews 11:1 (NIV) is the very next verse: "Now faith is being sure of what we hope for and certain of what we do not see." Many in the church know about this verse for the meeting of their needs, but to put it in the correct context of scripture, this verse is talking about *faith* for receiving our *full* salvation of mind/soul. "*Faith* is the *assurance* [freedom from doubt] of things *hoped* for [expected]" (Heb. 11:1, NASB, emphasis mine). Through *the patience of faith*, we must be prepared and expecting this to come about!

Let me make it very clear: we will not enter into the *fullness* of God unless we have *faith* and *patience* for this to take place in us! Faith simply put is "believing God for whatever He has said is ours to receive!" Whatever we seek after, we will find, whether it is the things of the world or the things that God has promised us. There is no greater hope or destiny for us than to receive our *full* salvation that Jesus died to give us!

The whole chapter of Hebrews 11 is called the *faith* chapter, but faith for what? To receive the riches of the world so that we can die, then give them to another? I think not! The primary gift of faith is so that we can believe God for something that is much bigger than what we could receive through our own works and strength.

> For we have become partners [shares] of Christ, "if" only we hold our first confidence [faith] firm to the end.... And we want each one of you to show the same diligence so as to realize the *full assurance of hope* to the very end, so that you may not become sluggish, but imitators of those who *through faith and patience inherit the promises* [becoming sons of God]. (Heb. 3:14, 6:11–12, NRSV, emphasis mine)

Now is the time for us to walk in the Spirit through faith, not obeying the lust of the flesh and the carnal mind. We must understand that there are three realms in the earth that we can choose to walk in and eat of every day, just as there were three trees to eat from in the Garden of Eden. The first tree was all the trees of the garden, the second was the tree of life, and the third was the tree of the knowledge of good and evil.

These three kinds of trees stand for *three kinds of men* that walk the earth today: the natural fleshly man, the soulish carnal man, and the spiritual man. The spirit is the realm of God consciousness, the soul is the realm of self-consciousness, and the body is the realm of sense consciousness. We must come to see that we can live out of either realm at all times by our choosing. For *now* we live and move in the Spirit realm and can eat and drink freely of God's Spirit at all times to stay strong in Him; it is our choice! Seek Him with all your heart, and go into the *high places* of the Spirit, for the heavens have been opened to us now!

The Heavens Are Now Open

> Now it came about when all the people were baptized, that Jesus also was baptized, and while He was praying, *heaven was opened*, and the Holy Spirit descended upon Him in bodily form like a dove, and a voice came out of heaven, "Thou art My beloved Son, in Thee I am well-pleased"
>
> —Luke 3:21–22 (NASB), emphasis mine

> And after He had sent the multitudes away, *He went up to the mountain by Himself to pray*, and when it was evening, *He was there alone.*
>
> —Matthew 14:23 (NASB), emphasis mine

Heaven, the spirit realm, was opened to Jesus so that He could ascend and descend freely at anytime that He needed to, to receive strength and wisdom from the Father. Jesus "went up to the mountain by Himself to pray," even as we are called to do in the spirit realm. Jesus lived both out of the spirit realm and the physical realm at the same time. "And no man hath ascended up to heaven, but he that came down from heaven, even the Son of man *which is in heaven*" (John 3:13, KJV, emphasis mine). Listen to what this verse is saying. Jesus is *in* heaven as He is *standing upon* the earth! Jesus knew that He must only drink spiritually from the Father; this is the realm of life. The same can be true for us when we are saved and filled with the Holy Spirit. We have a direct connection with God in the spirit and can live out of both realms at the same time, receiving our strength and wisdom from God. Paul said in Ephesians 2:6 (emphasis mine), "And [Jesus] *raised us up with Him* [in Spirit], and seated us with Him *in* the heavenly places, in Christ Jesus." Most Christians are waiting to go to heaven, but the truth of the matter is we can have heaven *now* on earth! God's presence is what makes heaven, heaven. *"In His presence is fullness of joy!"* If God's presence were not there, it would be hell no matter how nice it was. Take for example movie stars. They have the best of everything, yet many of their lives are a living hell because God's presence is not manifested in their lives. Or you could find a street person living in a cardboard shack with the presence of God, and it would be like heaven. Why? Because he has learned to live out of the realm of God! If we are going to make it through these days ahead, we too must learn to live out of the realm of the Spirit of God and get our strength and joy from Him daily. "If we live 'in' the Spirit, *let us also walk 'in' the Spirit*" (Gal. 5:25, KJV, emphasis mine).

Paul Mueller wrote the following article about the open heavens:

> As overcomers, we are called to ascend in the Spirit to the high places in God. This means that we shall ascend

to the highest of the heavens, which is the realm of the Spirit of God. But let us consider further the truth of ascending saints. When Jesus was calling His disciples, Philip brought Nathanael to Him. Jesus "saw" Nathanael coming, discerned his manner of life, and declared him to be, *"An Israelite indeed, in whom is no guile!"* Nathanael then acknowledged Jesus as the Son of God, and the King of Israel. *"Jesus answered and said unto him, because I said unto thee, I saw thee under the fig tree, believest thou?* **Thou shalt see greater things than these.** *And he saith unto him, Verily, verily, I say unto you, Hereafter* **ye shall see heaven open**, *and the angels of God ascending and descending upon the Son of man."* (John 1: *50–51*)

We are now seeing those *"greater things!* " This is another period designated as *"hereafter!"* It is the time when the heavens are open, and the angels of God are ascending and descending upon the Son of man. The word "angels," is derived from a Greek word, "aggelos," and means a messenger. There may be those in limited Christian experience who will see this as only being angels in the strict sense of the word. They cannot see themselves ascending and descending upon the Son of man. According to their limited faith and vision, only angels have that power and authority. And according to their faith, so be it unto them. God has given each of us the necessary faith and understanding according to our foreordained walk in Him. But my faith tells me that I have every right and privilege to ascend in the spirit as an angel or messenger of God, just as you do. And we shall ascend upon the Son of man until Father's purposes for us and His creation are completely fulfilled.

There is a further understanding of this word "angels," and that is that our spirits are the "angels" that ascend upon the Son of man. Obviously, our bodies cannot ascend into the realm of spirit, for they have not yet been changed and glorified. But our spirits ascend and descend upon the Son of man, just as Jesus foretold. *Our spirits, when in union with Christ (see John 3:13), can, and do, ascend to the realm of God's Spirit to commune with Him.* This is how you and I became sons of God. As sons of God and members of God's Christ, we have been given the authority to ascend and descend upon the Son of man. When we are joined to the Spirit of the Lord, we are one Spirit. Each of us then ascends in the Spirit to the throne of God, there to become one anointed, Christ body. There, in the Spirit, we commune with Him and receive His Truth. This is the fulfillment of Heb. 10:25! This is *"the assembling of ourselves together"* that we are not to forsake. When we ascend in the Spirit to commune with God in the spirit, we are thus fulfilling *"the greater things than these,"* that Jesus promised Nathanael. And our finite minds cannot possibly comprehend the many, spiritual wonders we shall yet see and receive as we continue to ascend and descend upon the Son of man.

Christ is the "ladder" to the realm of the Spirit. It is impossible for any one to come up by any other way. Not one person of Adam's lineage shall come unto the Father, except by Christ. (John 14:6) Christ is our access, our ladder! Use Him frequently! Call upon Him regularly! Take advantage of the glorious privilege we have in Christ! Forsake not the assembling of yourselves together! Gather together in Christ, by the Spirit, with all His saints of both heaven and earth. Vast distances may separate us from a literal gathering, but the Lord is gathering us together *by His Spirit*. We are one Spirit in Christ! He is molding and shaping us so that we also shall be of one faith! *The open heavens are before us!* The kingdom of God is at hand! As we ascend in the Spirit, we are seeing the throne of God and the dominion of His kingdom that is coming to earth. We shall also hear the new word of the kingdom that He would speak to us. We are being changed by the glory of His presence that permeates the Holiest of all! And that glory shall fill us to overflowing, transforming us within and without!

Six thousand years after Adam, we have abundant proof that the carnal, Adamic nature in all mankind is responsible for the conglomerate, Babylon religious systems we have today. Thousands of religious denominations, as well as Eastern religions, were created to make it possible for the carnal man to ascend without Christ. Through devious and carnal means, fallen Adam has sought to ascend the hill of the Lord in his own strength and authority. "He" even created religious denominations to make that possible. But, the Lord knew what was in him when He created Adam, so He set His plan in motion, a plan that would thwart Adam's plan and establish righteousness in the earth. And as sons of God, elect and chosen as His overcomers, we are called to ascend the hill of the Lord in Christ, thus overcoming and defeating the self-centered purposes of the carnal will and mind of fallen Adam.

Long centuries ago, God gave the vision of Christ, the ladder, to Jacob. As he laid down to sleep one night, *"he dreamed, and behold, a ladder set up on the earth, and the top of it reached to heaven; and behold, the angels of God ascending and descending on it. And, behold, the Lord stood above it, and said, I am the Lord God of Abraham thy father, and the God of Isaac."* (Gen. 28:12–13) The Lord then proceeded to make a covenant with Jacob. The heavens were opened for Jacob, and he could "see" the Lord God of his fathers, Abraham and Isaac. The ladder was set up on earth to indicate to Jacob that he had access to the heavenlies in and through Christ. And when the Lord finished giving His word and His covenant to him, Jacob knew that he had been in the presence of God. When he awoke, he said, *"Surely the Lord is in this place, and I knew it not. And he was afraid, and said, How dreadful is this place! This is none other but the house of God, and this is the gate of heaven."* (Vs. 16–17)

Beloved, we are *"the house of God!"* This is not a house made with hands; nor is this house administered by man, or governed by man's creeds and doctrines. God speaks in this house, not man! This is an eternal house in the heavens, to be seen only in the Spirit. We have found *"the gate of heaven!"* The gate of heaven is Christ! He is the gate or ladder that brings us to the Father and to His throne in the heavenlies. God is revealed and seen at the top of this ladder! But no man can see Him and live! The old, carnal man of the flesh must die completely so the new man of the spirit can be manifested. This is the path of our transformation! When we ascend in the Spirit, we are using Christ, the ladder, to approach our Father and His throne. When we ascend in the Spirit to the highest of the heavens, we shall see that we dwell securely in the house of the Lord.

WHEN GOD'S SHEKINAH WALKS THE EARTH

I heard a loud voice from the throne say, "See! God's
Sh'khinah is with mankind, and he will live with them.
They will be his people, and he himself, God-with-
them, will be their God."

—Revelation 21:3 (CJB)

W e are entering the most exciting time in all of human history to be alive, when God walks the earth in His manifest presence. What will all this look like? We cannot be for sure about everything, but this we know of: in the book of Revelation 21:4–5, there will be no more tears, death, mourning, crying, or pain for He is making all things new. These verses may seem like a fairy tale to many and impossible to come to pass, but even as the impossibility of the resurrection took place, so will these words because our God is faithful to His word. Also he said, "Write, 'These words are true and trustworthy!'" (Rev. 21:5, CJB). In other words, *take it to the bank; these words will be fulfilled in their time!*

What will these days—or should I say people—look like in the day of the Lord, as we are clothed with God's Shekinah glory even as Adam and Jesus were? We have come into a time where the reaping of all that has been sown will be reaped for good and evil. We are seeing the evil in people come into the complete likeness of the evil one; also we are going to see people come into the complete likeness of Jesus, manifesting His Shekinah for all to see.

These chosen ones are going to display God's "abiding manifest glory" for that is what Shekinah means. I see a day coming when God's Shekinah glory will manifest on the overcomers for all to see with the naked eye. Most will run to the Lord and repent of their former lives because of this. The glory will manifest when God wills it to; it could be in an airport, office, church, or a home. Just as the Lord manifested His glory after the resurrection to only five hundred people, it will be to His choosing. He could have shown Himself to the whole of Israel at that time and all would have been saved, but He wants to work through a body of people that are called to be like Him. That is the key! If you are saved from your sin, you have the privilege and high calling to be a part of this great adventure to restore mankind and the world back to God.

A People Likened unto Him

Beloved, now we are children of God, and it has not appeared as yet what we will be. We know that when He appears, we will be like Him, because we will see Him just as He is.

—1 John 3:2 (NASU)

I know that it's hard for us who are still living in this frail human body to imagine that we will one day walk in the full likeness of Jesus and abide in His Shekinah glory. Yet the truth of the matter is, we already do abide in the glory—we just don't understand it! For instance, we get a good snapshot of this when Israel was abiding around the tabernacle of God's Shekinah in the wilderness. When the Lord had Moses build the tabernacle in the wilderness, it shows us that when we are walking through a desert (spiritually speaking), God's glory is with us. We may be living in a seemingly dry and difficult time, yet there is a glory there that we could not have unless we walked through the desert.

The Promised Land lies on the other side of the wilderness experience. Just as most of Israel who started out in the desert died there, so has been the story of the church because most quit following Him in the difficult times. Yet there will be a generation that will not quit and will come into all the promises of God for their life and for the world. The glory was in the wilderness for them at that time, but they did not have to stay there for forty years. Once we learn the blessing of His presence in difficult days, we can enjoy the journey until we pass through the wilderness. We are not to stay there forever, but pass through a learning curve, thank God!

For thirteen years of my life, I passed through the wilderness of not knowing why God had sent us to Florida to live. There were many excruciating years of not having enough money, people rising up against me, not having any close Christian fellowship, or many ministry opportunities. Yet the Lord's presence and the revelation of His word were truly glorious in those days of drawing closer to the Lord. No, I would not want to go back through the wilderness, but I am very thankful for it even when it seemed as if it would never end, or it felt like God was mad at me. These were the days that I got to know myself, and better yet, I got to know the Lord more! He promised me that I would know Him more, and I did, and I continue growing in Him daily.

We could study the lives of many men in the Bible who had to go through the wilderness to get to their place of destiny. The likes of Abraham, Moses, David, Jesus, and Paul, to name a few. Yet this is the very thing that God used to forge these into great men of God. The good thing is, once they got through, they never had to go back through the wilderness experience again. We all must learn the lesson on how faithful God is in the midst of our trials of life; there is no quick and easy way of leaning this but through the passage of time. Jesus is the only one who got through the wilderness in forty days having defeated the enemy hands down. It took Moses forty years to learn what he needed. For the rest of us, it may take many years to learn and grow; just know that the wilderness is a good and safe place to be in the will of God. I can tell you the quickest way through is to yield yourself completely to the will of God and praise Him through it, no matter what you may be feeling. Also, ask God to put someone in your life to mentor you who has already gone through the wilderness and has passed the tests, and even better yet, have a companion to walk with you through it.

The thing we must know is to seek God's presence in the midst of all the human emotions. When Israel was in the wilderness, God's presence was right there to protect them from the sun with a cloud of glory by day and a fiery cloud by night to keep them warm. No enemies or wild beasts attacked the people while God's glory was in their midst. We do not have to fear the wilderness experience; we must only face it with true living faith that God is doing a work in us. That will one day prepare us for our kingdom work for eternity; we must stop agonizing our present circumstances and start rejoicing that God is doing a great work in us for His glory.

The Blessed of God

There was a time when God's Shekinah dwelt in just one home—the home of Obed-edom. For three months, God's presence rested there before David came and took the Ark of the Covenant to Jerusalem. Yet the Bible speaks very well of Obed-edom in 1 Chronicles 26:5 (NASU): "God had indeed blessed him." Who would not want this spoken over their life? For Obed-edom, God's presence made the difference that brought God's blessings many fold to his family to know and serve God.

First Chronicles 26:6 says this about Obed-edom's sons: "For they were mighty men of valor." Verse 8 says, "All these were of the sons of Obed-edom; they and their sons and their relatives were able men with strength for the service, 62 from Obed-edom." Verse 12 says, "To these divisions of the gatekeepers, the chief men, were given duties like their relatives to minister in the house of the Lord." There is no higher call given unto men than to minister unto the Lord. The story does not end there; it gets better! In verse 15, we are told that their lot fell unto them to be gatekeepers over the storehouse in the house of the Lord. I am not sure what all that means today, but it sounds like a pretty important position given by God.

Gatekeepers were also watchmen on the wall. They were trusted officials in the servant role of protecting the Lord's house; they were stationed at all four gates. They also were appointed and taught others around them to guard the gate as well. Their hearts were fully committed to the Lord's will. Today's gatekeepers pray for revival and encourage others to get ready for the glory of the Lord to come. They also were in charge of the temple and items in the treasuries of the House of the Lord. This is what you and I are called to do if we are people passionate for His presence.

Obed-Edom: the Bless Man of God

Thus the ark of God remained with the family of
Obed-edom in his house three months; and the
Lord blessed the family of Obed-edom with all
that he had.

—1 Chronicles 13:14 (NASU)

If you will remember the story of Obed-edom, the Ark of the Covenant was taken by the Philistines in war, and David wanted to get it back to Jerusalem. So David sent men out with oxen and a new cart to bring it home to him, but that was not God's prescribed way of doing things with His presence. The oxen stumbled, and a man named Uzza reached out and grabbed them and was smitten by the Lord for disrespecting His presence. Because there was only one way to carry the presence of God, and that was on the shoulders of men. Nothing has changed today. God's people are still called to carry the Shekinah of God together in their hearts.

Now David was terrified of the Lord for doing this, so he put the ark of the Lord in the house of Obed-edom for safekeeping until he could figure out how to get it back to Jerusalem. In the meantime, Obed-edom's life is about to change. He and his family are going to become lovers and chasers of God for the rest of their life, for they fell in love with the presence of the Lord. Because they honored His presence, the Lord in turn honored them with blessing his household. I believe the same is true today. If we will be seekers of God's presence because we love Him and love to spend time with Him, He will also honor us with His presence, with more joy, peace, strength, love, and with whatever provisions we may have need of.

David soon heard that Obed-edom's house was being blessed by the presence of the Lord, and he also wanted that blessing in Jerusalem. So he prepared a place for it: "And they brought in the ark of God and placed it inside the tent which David had pitched for it, and they offered burnt offerings and peace offerings before God" (1 Chron. 16:1, NASU). If we want to host the presence of the Lord, we must also prepare our hearts for His abiding presence in our life. Simply, we must hunger and ask Him for His presence, then we must forsake anything that might offend Him so that we can make quality time to sit and soak in His perfect love. The more we eat of the Lord, the more we need, and the more we will want of Him!

Once Obed-edom had the presence of the Lord in his life, there was no way that he was not going to run after the Lord. He and his family left their house to follow the glory of the Lord to Jerusalem. Now this was a personal thing to him, not just some box in his house. He was now forming a relationship with the Lord, and nobody could take that away from him. So he moved. I don't know if he sold everything that he had or if David blessed him with a place of his own for looking after the ark, but he did follow the presence of God, this we know.

The next time we find Obed-edom's name in the scriptures is next to the ark again in Jerusalem. "Obed-edom and Jehiah also were gatekeepers for the ark" (1 Chron. 15:24, NASU). And again we read in 1 Chronicles 16:5, "Obed-edom and Jeiel, with musical instruments, harps, lyres." This man could not get enough of God and would not be stopped from seeking the Lord with all his heart. I could see this man singing and dancing before the Lord with David. They were lovesick! Obed-edom is little known by the church today, yet he is truly one of the great seekers of God's presence in all of scripture. I do look forward to meeting this man in glory someday, and me thinks I shall find him worshipping on the throne.

As I wrote before, Obed-edom did not go to Jerusalem alone, oh no. He brought sixty-eight of his relatives with him. Most of them would be found worshipping before the ark of God's presence also. "So he left Asaph and his relatives there before the ark of the covenant of the Lord to minister before the ark continually, as every day's work required; and Obed-edom with his 68 relatives" (1 Chron. 16:37–38, NASU).

Hallelujah! This is the story of a man who truly loved God with all his heart and is forever forged into the word of God because he was a man of the Shekinah. What will be written of our life when all is said and done? Are you a seeker of God's presence, or are you satisfied with the "just going through the motions" of tradition and religion?

A Servant of Edom

After years of wondering why God would allow His glory to stay in this one house, the house of Obed-edom, I feel I have some revelation as to why. You see, Obed-edom's name means "servant of Edom," in other words, "servant of the flesh." You see, if we understand this prophetically, Edom's name is synonymous with the fleshly religious church that wants nothing to do with the moving of the Holy Spirit. In fact, they oppose Him greatly to the point of even hindering God's people when they try to flow with the Spirit of God. The Lord Himself said that He will do away with this type of opposition spirit in the church.

> "Will I not on that day," declares the Lord, "Destroy wise men from Edom and understanding from the mountain of Esau?" (Obad. 1:8, NASU)

The Edomites are the sons of Esau who always oppose the ways of God. He will soon do away with this obstinate spirit in the church through a movement with power. Not through the destruction of a people, but the spirit that is controlling them. The Lord goes on to say in verse 21, "The deliverers will ascend Mount Zion to judge the mountain of Esau, and the kingdom will be the Lord's." God's deliverers are His judges, the sons of God that ascend into kingdom power and will do away with this religious spirit that is now controlling most churches today. These Edomites are going to turn to the Lord in this next great move of God that is soon to break out on the earth. God's love, mercy, and kindness will win over the hardest of hearts.

The story of Obed-edom is soon going to be the story of all people that are in the church and are controlled by a religious spirit to seek the heart of God as Obed-edom did. God's presence will win them over! In fact, they will become some of the most dedicated to seeking the heart of God. They and their relatives are about to get turned on to God like nothing we have ever seen before!

God's Shekinah Walks the Earth in You

I heard a loud voice from the throne say, "See! God's
Sh'khinah is with mankind, and he will live with them.
They will be his people, and he himself, God-with-
them, will be their God."

—Revelation 21:3 (cjb)

What will it look like when God's Shekinah walks the earth
in and through us? Can you see a world without sin, death,
poverty, and lack? A place where only righteousness reigns and
the whole earth has come into the liberty of the sons of God?
This is where the first world of sin and death have passed away,
and now the kingdom age has come. We are being prepared to
rule and reign with Jesus in this new world and the universe
forever. This is why we must be tried over and over as gold is, to
get out of us all that is not of Him so we can be entrusted with
His power, glory, and likeness.

The good thing about God is we do not have to wait for the
millennium to come to be anointed and used for His purposes;
we must find a place now to let His glory shine through us. It's
not just going to happen; we also must find the geographical
place in the world where the will of God is for us. We are the
carriers of His glory, and now is the time to release the Shekinah
into the hearts of those He has been preparing.

One day soon, the Shekinah glory is going to fall upon His chosen ones that are the first fruits of the harvest. These are the harvesters of the kingdom, the sons of God that will be the seed planters to bring in the great harvest of mankind. "And the field is the world; and as for the good seed, these are the sons of the kingdom" (Matt. 13:38, NASU). I believe if you are reading this, it is because you are called of God to be a part of the great harvest machine that is soon to go through the nation unhindered. Seek Him, seek the Shekinah of God with all your heart!

SEEING IS BELIEVING

"What do you want me to do for you?" Jesus asked him.
The blind man said, "Rabbi, *I want to see*."

—Mark 10:51 (NIV), emphasis mine

Thankfully, I was not born physically blind nor have I ever been blind, but when I see a blind person, my heart immediately goes out to them. I wonder what their dark world must be like. How does their imagination see everything, not knowing the colors of the sky, grass, trees, etc.? Can they even imagine the beauty of a person or an animal that is beside them? How terrible it must be to be blind to God's physical creation!

But to be honest with you, we were all born blind spiritually, whether we know it or not, which is far worse! For us to see with the eyes of our spirit is far more important than for us to see with our physical eyes. It was said of blind hymn writer George Matheson that God made him blind so that he could see clearly in the spirit, to become a guide to spiritually blind men. We must be like the blind man that came to Jesus and cried out to Him, "I want to see!" How desperately a blind man must want to see. When they know that Jesus can heal them, they will cry out like blind Bartimaeus continued crying out to Jesus, "Have mercy on me!" The problem with most people is that they are like the Pharisees; they do not even *know* that they are spiritually blind!

> And Jesus said, "For judgment I came into this world, that those *who do not see may see* [see spiritually]; and that those who see may become blind." Those of the Pharisees who were with Him heard these things, and said to Him, "*We are not blind too, are we?*" Jesus said to them, "If you were blind, you would have no sin; *but since you say, 'We see,'* your sin remains." (John 9:39–41, NASB, emphasis mine)

When we understand that we were lost in spiritual darkness is when we are having our spiritual eyes opened. The average person does not even realize there is a spirit realm of God around them to be reckoned with, much less one that they can see and enter into. God has created man to dwell in both the natural and spirit realms at the same time. The realm that I am writing about is the realm of light and truth! We are living in two realms at one time, one of light/truth and one of darkness/deception. Jesus desires to open our spiritual vision and understanding so that we might see what is hidden in the darkness of our *own* soul. For in our soul darkness hides, and it blocks our understanding of knowing the truth. This is why many Christians cannot go beyond the salvation experience for they do not want to deal with the darkness of their own soul.

Jesus said to the church in Laodicea, "I advise you to buy from Me gold refined by fire... and eye salve to anoint your eyes, *that you may see*" (Rev. 3:18, NASB, emphasis mine). Oh yes, make no mistake about it. Jesus wants us to see and understand spiritual truth clearly. When Paul the apostle was thrown off his horse, he was blinded by the truth of Jesus Christ for the light/truth revealed his blindness. We must see ourselves ignorant of the truth before we can know the truth, so it then can change us.

One day I was in my office, and Jesus came in spirit form and sat down in front of my desk. I said to Him, "Why can't I see you with my natural eyes?" He said, "Because you can see with your spiritual eyes." It then dawned on me that we could truly see with the eyes of our heart into the spirit world.

> A woman named Rose Crawford had been blind for 50 years. "I just can't believe it!" She gasped as the doctor lifted the bandages from her eyes after her recovery from delicate surgery in an Ontario hospital. She wept for joy when for the first time in her life a dazzling and beautiful world of form and color greeted eyes that now were able to see. The amazing thing about the story, however, is that 20 years of her blindness had been unnecessary. She didn't know that surgical techniques had been developed, and that an operation could have restored her vision at the age of 30. The doctor said, "She just figured there was nothing that could be done about her condition. Much of her life could have been different."

But no one told her about the wonderful advances in eye surgery?

I think about many Christians that have a very dim view of spiritual things. They have need of spiritual eye salve being applied to their eyes so that they can see the things of the Spirit. Or there are those that have tunnel vision, only seeing what others have taught them about God, when in fact, Jesus wants to teach us by His Spirit the deep things of God. "If so be that *ye have heard him*, and have been *taught by him*, as the *truth is in Jesus*" (Eph. 4:21, KJV, emphasis mine). Many Christians do not even know what they are missing or how much they have lost in true spiritual riches because of their limited view! Many Christians think that they can see 20/20 in the spirit realm because they are saved, salvation being the only revelation they have ever had, not realizing that they are only seeing the "in part realm" of the truths of God.

We must understand that God is bigger than the universe, and that "truth" is as vast as the universe itself, never to be fully understood this side of eternity. This is why our daily prayer must be "*I pray that the eyes of your heart may be enlightened [opened], so that you may know* what is the hope of His calling, what are the riches of the glory of His inheritance in the saints" (Eph. 1:18, NASB, emphasis mine). This is what I mean by us having our spiritual eyes opened: *when we know and understand the truths of God's word by us having an on-going revelation of the person of Jesus Christ*. Paul said, "For I neither received it [the truth] from man, nor was I taught it, *but I received it through a revelation of Jesus Christ*" (Gal. 1:12, NASB, emphasis mine).

Now That's Something to See

People like to see many things in the earth like the Grand Canyon, New York City, Paris, etc. When they have seen it with their own eyes, they say, "Wasn't that something to see!" But it was only a natural experience lasting a very short time, and they probably never gained any spiritual insight from what they were seeing.

I was on a missionary trip in northern India and was staying in the Himalayan Mountains. We were there for one week, and the sky was cloudy every day. The people living there would point to the mountains and tell me that the third-highest mountain in the world was behind the clouds. They would then show me pictures of what the mountain looked like when it wasn't cloudy. In my mind's eye, I could not imagine what a twenty-nine-thousand-foot mountain peak would look like.

When I was a young boy, my dad took me to the Rocky Mountains of Colorado to see fourteen-thousand-foot peaks, and I remembered being so disappointed that they were so little! Now I was on the other side of the earth, and the tallest mountains in the world were all around me, yet I could not see them! So I prayed and asked the Lord to show me these mountains. The very last day we were there, I woke up at 5:00 a.m. to see if the sky had cleared, and it had! I then proceeded to the top of the roof where there was a viewing platform. I looked to where the people had pointed, and sure enough, there was the tallest mountain that I had ever seen. It literally took my breath away, as if I was looking at God Himself! I was not disappointed in the least bit!

I have written all this to say this: As great as it was for me to see the wonders of the earth, it never changed me one bit! But when I have seen the many facets of God's word, I have been changed from within. Every time spiritual truth is revealed to me, I am breathless! There have been times when all I could do was shout and praise God as truth was opened to me. There were times when I would have to lie on the floor because all my strength had left me, as it did Daniel when he had seen great visions. "So I was left alone and saw this great vision; yet no strength was left in me, for my natural color turned to a deathly pallor, and I retained no strength" (Dan. 10:8, NASB).

It is far more important for us to see and understand spiritual truth than it is for us to travel the world over and see things that will have no spiritual impact on our eternal destiny. Once we see in our spirit the wonder of wonders of God's word, we will be changed little by little into the likeness of Jesus, for He is the beginner and finisher of our faith. It is only by seeing Him that we are changed. "Beloved, now we are children of God, and it has not appeared as yet what we shall be. We know that, *when He appears* [when He is seen in spirit], we shall be like Him, *because we shall see Him just as He is*" (1 John 3:2, NASB, emphasis mine). We must now see Him in the word and Spirit to be changed into His likeness, by going from glory level of truth to glory level. Then we too can say, "Seeing is truly believing!" As the angel in the book of Revelation said to John, "Come and see!"

COME TO THE GARDEN

So we fix our eyes not on what is seen, but on what is unseen. For what is seen is temporary, *but what is unseen is eternal* (2 Cor. 4:18, NIV, emphasis mine).

Blinded

> Then the angel of the LORD appeared to the woman,
> and said to her, "Behold now, you are barren and have
> borne no children, but you shall conceive and give birth
> to a son [Samson].... And *he shall begin to deliver Israel*
> from the hands of the Philistines."
>
> —Judges 13:3, 5b (NASB), emphasis mine

The story of Samson is one of great wonder and awe at his power and courage and one of sadness and sorrow at his lack of character. Samson's calling is much like the sons of God; they are called to be deliverers! Deliverers of people that are caught in the bondage of sin and darkness. Much of Samson's life is a mystery to me. Why did God call him? Why did God allow him to marry a Philistine girl when other Jewish men could not? And why did his death have to be by his own hands? I do not pretend to have the answers, but there are many great truths about his life that we must glean if we are to be the deliverers that God has called us to be.

Much like the life of Jesus, Samson was born and raised from birth to be a deliverer of the people. For this alone was he born, and as far as we know, he did not have any children. Samson had no other calling in his life but to be a deliverer of the people. Even though God anointed him in strange ways, he was still a deliverer of the people through his own personal problems. What he did *was not* for the nation of Israel, but for his *own* revenge. And for this reason, we should also fight the Philistines in our own life! The Philistines in scripture always represent the "the fleshly carnal nature" that wars against us *daily*, even as the Philistine Delilah vexed Samson daily. Delilah's name means "long hair." In other words, by her lies and seduction, she seduced him so much that he gave his whole heart over to her (see Judges 16:16). We must be careful of this Delilah that is living in *our* flesh; she is a "whore" that is living in us to seduce us by her cunning ways! The Philistine spirit is living *in* our flesh, and we must overcome it, or Delilah [the flesh] will put us spiritually to sleep and torment and terrorize us as she terrorized Samson! "Then *she lulled him to sleep* on her knees, and called for a man and had him shave off the seven locks of his head. *Then she began to torment him*, and his strength left him" (Judges 16:19, NKJV, emphasis mine). Flirting with the flesh will put us to sleep, and we will lose our spiritual strength, our joy of salvation.

It is interesting to note that the nation of Israel is today back in her Promised Land of the Middle East as she was in Samson's day. And the Philistines are *terrorizing* them once again! Why do I say this? The West Bank and the Gaza Strip is the Palestinian occupied territory, the same ancient land that the Philistines occupied thousands of years ago! The same evil spirits that attacked Israel then are now attacking Israel today. The name *Palestine* comes from the word *Philistine*; look at their close spelling. This is not by chance, for the Roman government that ruled over the land of Philistine changed the name to Palestine! Prophetically, what does this say to us? That we, as the church, are under the same *terrorist attacks* as Israel is in the natural, but it is by our own "fleshly nature" that is warring *in* us. We, like Israel, cannot afford to exchange our spiritual land (that we have gained through our personal warrings) for any type of peace treaty with the flesh; we must fight for complete victory over our flesh! Even though the flesh (the beast system) is becoming stronger in the earth than ever before, we must overcome it through God's grace. For there will *never* be a lasting peace treaty between our spirit man and fleshly nature.

Many people point to Samson and say that he failed God because he was with strange women. This is so, but the truth of the matter is, God still used him in his failure to deliver the children of Israel! When Samson wanted to marry a Philistine woman, his father did not want him to do so. But God was behind the marriage all the time. "But his father and his mother knew not that it was of the LORD, that he sought an occasion against the Philistines: for at that time the Philistines had dominion over Israel" (Judges 14:4, KJV). God's ways are not our ways; He is able to use many different means of deliverance in our own life and the life of a nation. We must not put God in a box and say what He can and cannot do! My personal feeling about Samson is that he was not a strong man in the natural or in the spirit. He was in fact a weakling, for this is the only thing that would have given God the glory in his victories.

The truth of the matter is Samson lost his way when he began playing around with his anointing and falsely thinking he was invincible against the Philistines (the flesh). This should be a clear warning to us not to play around with the things of the flesh. Yes, God's word and anointing is greater than anything the enemy has, yet God will leave us with the Philistines (the flesh) if we do not respect the anointing that is in us!

> And she said, "The Philistines are upon you, Samson!" And he awoke from his sleep and said, "I will go out as at other times and shake myself free." *But he did not know that the* LORD *had departed from him.* Then the Philistines seized him and *gouged out his eyes; and they brought him down to Gaza* and bound him with bronze chains, and he was a grinder in the prison. (Judges 16:20–21, NASB, emphasis mine)

Please hear me. The flesh will *blind us* spiritually to the deeper things of God, as it did Samson, if we continue to play around with it, for we are in danger of giving our heart over to it as Samson did! "So he told her all that was in his heart and then she *tormented* him!" (See verses 17 and 19). We must only give our heart over to the Lord for He is the only worthy one to be trusted! Jesus is now offering us eye salve so that we might see clearly into the deeper things of God. Let us now run unto Him so that we might see clearly!

DON'T BE TAKEN PRISONER!

It was for freedom that Christ set us free; *therefore*
keep standing firm and do not be subject again to
a yoke of slavery.

—Galatians 5:1 (NASB)

There are different types of prisons in life. Many times we only think of a jail as being a prison to keep bad people behind bars from hurting others. Now they have been restricted from their everyday freedoms that we all have learned to enjoy. But there are also prisons of our own making, like alcohol, drugs, anger, fear, hatred, pornography, gambling, worry—and the list could go on and on. These are all prisons and addictions that want to keep us in bondage. Anything that we are addicted to, other than God, can become a prison for us because they restrict our freedom to know Jesus more. Only God can help free us from these addictions. But there is one other prison or addiction that we forget about; it's called "religion."

Paul's letter to the Galatian church was on this very subject of being in bondage or imprisoned to programmed religion—the "Law." This was restricting their freedom of moving on with God into greater maturity and revelations of His word and Spirit.

God wants us free to follow Him and not be hindered or under the control of any group of people or church denominations that don't want to go higher into the things of God. In fact, Jesus told us in Matthew 18:7–8 to "cut off" any part of the "body," "the church," that would be a stumbling block to us from growing into His full likeness. *"It was for freedom that Christ set us free!"*

> *See to it that no one takes you captive* [prisoner] through hollow [shallow] and *deceptive philosophy* [doctrines], *which depends on human tradition* and the basic principles of this world rather than on Christ. *For in Christ all the fullness of the Deity lives in bodily form, and you have been given fullness in Christ,* who is the head over every power and authority. (Col. 2:8–10, NIV, emphasis mine)

If we already have been given the *fullness* of God through Jesus Christ, what are we doing settling for anything less than *all* that He is? We must chase after His fullness in order to obtain it! God has put a great challenge before us that we might be like Him. If anything tries to stop or hinder us from this calling, we must fight against it to go higher unto the transformation of our bodies. We are not to be *taken captive or held prisoner* by anyone's denominational traditions.

As a small boy, I was raised in the Lutheran church. Lutheranism was all that I knew about God and the truths of the Bible. As far as I knew, everyone in the world believed as a Lutheran! Then one day I heard about "those Baptists" (this was the church that did not let their children go to dances). When I heard this, I thought, *Thank God I'm Lutheran! They don't care if I go to the dance or not!* It did not matter what God thought about dancing as long the Lutherans okayed it, and it was all right with me. My mind had been controlled by Lutheran doctrines that I had learned as a little boy; the word and Spirit of God did not control my mind.

Most Christians faithfully attend their particular church year after year, and many attend the same church for their entire lifetime, believing that they are pleasing God. For some, this may be God's will for them to attend "their church" for a certain time in their lives, but never to settle down and say, "We have all there is, why leave?" As children, we attended elementary school, starting out in kindergarten. But how many of us would still like to be going to the same school, the same grade, and to have the same teacher year after year? None of us! Have you ever heard a kindergartner say, "I know how to read and write, just watch me!" Then as they begin to show you their writing skills, you notice that most of it is just scribbling on paper. Even though they believe they know how to do it, they are just fooling themselves because they have not yet matured in the educational process. This is how many Christians act in regard to knowing the deeper truths of God's word. They are just children in their understanding because they have not been fed solid food to become spiritually mature. They have not matured in their faith through the deeper teachings of God's word; they are, as the writer of Hebrews says, "babes in their understanding."

For though by this time you ought to be teachers, *you have need again for someone to teach you the elementary principles of the oracles [word] of God, and you have come to need milk [elementary teachings] and not solid food* [the deeper teachings of Christ]. For everyone who partakes only of milk is not accustomed to the word of righteousness, *for he is a babe.* But solid food is for the mature, who because of practice [growth] have their senses [spiritual understanding] trained to discern good [that which is valuable] and evil [that which is worthless]. *Therefore leaving the elementary teaching about the Christ, let us press on to maturity.* (Heb. 5:12–14, 6:1; NASB; emphasis mine)

We must press on to maturity; God will not instantly make us mature by snapping His fingers! He has given us His word, Spirit, and our life experiences to help change us and bring us to maturity through our obedience to Him. But if we stay in one church all our life, we cannot mature because no one pastor or church has all truth that is needed for us to grow. We must go where God leads us and press toward the high calling of God in Christ Jesus. Galatians 4:1–3 says, "Now I say, as long as the heir is a child [in understanding], he does not differ at all from a slave although he is owner of everything, *but he is under guardians and managers until the date [time] set by the father.* So also we, while we were children [infants], were held in bondage under the elemental [basic] things of the world [and church]."

In order for me to grow in the things of God, I had to leave the Lutheran church and press on to the calling of God for my life. Great pressure was placed upon me from old friends, relatives, family members, and two Lutheran ministers who tried to stop me from going forward into the call of God. Unknowingly, they wanted to imprison me to Lutheranism and have me turn around from the path of life that I was on and stay in the church because they thought this was right for my life. But if I had not left the church, I would have forfeited God's calling on my life. When God calls us to go higher with Him, we must leave the basic teachings of Christ and come out from under the yoke of elementary pastors and teachers. As spiritual children, we were "under guardians and managers" for a time by the will of the Father. But if we desire to be taught the deeper truths of Christ, we must come away from them to sit at the feet of Jesus, the great Teacher.

> And as for you, the anointing which you received from Him abides in you, and *you have no need for anyone to teach you; but as His anointing teaches you about all things, and is true and is not a lie,* and just as it has taught you, you abide in Him. (1 John 2:27, NASB, emphasis mine)

The elementary churches will always call us back down to their present level of teaching and revelation of the scriptures and will not allow us to go much beyond their understanding without attacking us and calling us a heretic. An elementary student does not understand high school material because the teaching is over their head, and they would be lost in it. So it is with the elementary Christians in the church; they just cannot comprehend it at this time, but they will later.

If God is calling you out of your present church, and you choose to stay in it because you are afraid of what people might say and do not want to rock the boat or change, then let me tell you as lovingly and clearly as I can write, *you are in a prison of religion*! The Lord will consider you as a coward in your time of judgment before Him (see Rev. 21:7–8). A prison is a place that restricts your freedom from going forward into what God has called you to be. As a Lutheran, I was taught that a person was born again through infant baptism. If I believed that I needed to receive Jesus into my heart and be baptized in water as a believer, they would have said I was a heretic and thrown me out. Even this basic teaching of being baptized in water as a believer was unknown to them because the spirit of religion was holding their mind prisoner to these strongholds of church doctrine.

This same thing has happened to many evangelical Christians that say they have the baptism of the Holy Spirit when they received Jesus as Savior into their heart. But when one of them receives the baptism of the Holy Spirit with the evidence of speaking in other tongues, they say, "That's of the devil, you're a heretic, go away from us!" Where people are in their present experience with Christ determines what they believe and receive from others through their lifetime. Most Baptists are Baptists because that is what they were brought up in, and so it is with other people's religious beliefs. If a person does not push into more of God by leaving the church that they are in (in God's timing), they will end up staying on that present level of spiritual understanding for the rest of their lives to the displeasure of heaven.

Pentecostal Christians are guilty of the same thing. Many believe that they have received everything that God has for them *because* they speak in tongues. Instead of using tongues as a tool and a stepping stone to press into more of the things of God, they totally stop seeking the greater revelations of the Lord. If anyone goes beyond where they are in their Christian walk, they also call them heretics because they cannot understand it. This cycle goes on and on from one religious generation to the next. It's a spiritual cycle and prison house to captivate us from going higher into the greater things of God!

When the Lord told me to resign from the Assemblies of God as a minister, I thought, *This couldn't be from God!* But when I finally obeyed Him, I felt as if I was a bird let out of a cage to fly for my first time! Then God began to teach me the greater truths of His word with many outside confirmations assuring me that I was hearing from Him. I could not have received these deeper truths in the church as a pastor because the people were not ready to receive them and would have thrown me out as a heretic. If we will obey God's leading, He will lead us into His great treasure house.

If you know in your heart that God is calling you to come out from the religious Babylonian systems of man, *come out from them and go higher in God!* "Come out of her, my people, that you may not participate in her sins and that you may not receive of her plagues" (Rev. 18:4, NASB). Obey Him, and He will lead you into greater things than you could ever imagine. We must see this higher walk of Christianity as a mountain climber does.

A climber always seeks a higher mountain than the pervious one; if we can see the top of the mountain, we can get there. Unless we put one foot in front of the other, we will not see what God has in store for our lives because we were fearful of the unknown. Our natural mind is not to be controlled by the spirits of this age, like anger, fear, lust, and worry. *"You formerly walked according to the course of this world,* according to the prince of the power of the air, of the spirit that is now working in the sons of disobedience" (Eph. 2:2, NASB, emphasis mine). Even as there are evil spirits controlling the people of the world, so there are religious spirits assigned to every denomination to keep the people in bondage to their traditions of man and to captivate them, keeping them from going higher into the things of God.

There is only one way for us to keep out of those religious prisons and for us to keep growing into the likeness of Jesus. It is found in Colossians 3:1–4 (emphasis mine): "If then you have been raised up with Christ, *keep seeking the things above, where Christ is,* seated at the right hand of God. *Set your mind on the things above, not on the things that are on earth.* For you have died and your life is hidden with Christ in God. When Christ, *who is our life,* is revealed, then you also will be revealed with Him in glory." We will not find the greater revelations of God in the mixture of man's religious programs. *We must hunger for more truth that is in Jesus alone.*

If we have been saved from above where Jesus is, should we not continually seek the things above where Christ is seated in the heavenlies? "And raised us up with Him, *and seated us with Him in the heavenly places*, in Christ Jesus" (Eph. 2:6, NASB, emphasis mine). If we are to come to full maturity in Christ, we must continually seek for a greater revelation of Him in the spirit where He is, and not the things below in the traditions of man. Greater truths will not be found in the elementary teachings of the church, but the Spirit of truth will give them unto us if we ask for them. "But when He, *the Spirit of truth, comes, He will guide you into all the truth*… He shall glorify Me; *for He shall take of Mine, and shall disclose [show] it to you*" (John 16:13–14, NASB, emphasis mine). Although walking in the "truth" is more than just knowing and doing certain doctrines. It is knowing the truth in our heart and being true to it, not living the lie of tradition and the deceptions of men that steal the greater truths of God from us. We must focus upward where Jesus is in order for us to get there. A mountain climber can only get to the top of the mountain when he is focusing upward! If we continue to focus upon the things below, we will be at best a carnal Christian. But when we focus our attention upward, we will be seeking His face! Paul clearly tells us to "*set your mind* on the things above!" Seeking the things above starts within our own mind and thoughts. "For he who comes to God must believe that He is, and that *He is a rewarder of those who seek Him*" (Heb. 11:6, NASB, emphasis mine). As we set our mind on seeking Him, He will reward us with the greater revelations of Himself, who is our *life*. Our life is hidden in Christ, and His *life* and presence is what we need most.

We Must Cleanse Ourselves First

Put to death, therefore, whatever belongs to your earthly
nature: sexual immorality, impurity, lust, evil desires and
greed, which is idolatry.

—Colossians 3:5 (NIV)

If it is our desire to be raised up with Jesus in great glory and
power when He is revealed, *we* must cleanse ourselves by putting
to death the way of the world, the flesh, and the devil in us. To
be dead to sin does not mean that we are not tempted anymore,
but that our spirit man has grown and matured stronger than the
man of sin in us, and we no longer have to obey its evil desires.
Even Jesus was tempted as we are, yet without sin. He struggled
with His fleshly mind in Gethsemane before His death, but His
spirit man was stronger than the flesh, and He could obey the
Father's will. "Abba! Father! All things are possible for Thee;
remove this cup from Me; *yet not what I will* [His fleshly will],
but what Thou wilt" (Mark 14:36, NASB, emphasis mine). Our
faith and trust will also grow in the Father's love with every test
that we pass and as we are being totally dependent upon Him to
bring us through each test victoriously. We then will grow into
the likeness of Jesus, even as we are growing older and wiser in
our physical body through our trials and life experiences.

> If a man *cleanses himself* from the latter [worldly and earthly things], he will be *an instrument for noble purposes, made holy, useful to the Master and prepared to do any good work* [the work of sonship]. (2 Tim. 2:21, NIV, emphasis mine)

The word tells us that we must cleanse ourselves; God is not going to wave a magic wand over us and say, "Now you are clean!" Our trials and life experiences are set up by God to help cleanse and prepare us for His coming glory; God is now using our life experiences to help us see where we are not like Him and where we need to be cleansed. But how can we cleanse ourselves? Does this mean that we just grit our teeth and say to ourselves, "I'm no longer going to sin?" Well, good luck! Because you're going to need it! God will help us in our daily battles as we submit them to Him. To think that we will ever be totally sinless in this life is wishful thinking, for no person has ever done it other than Jesus. The man of sin that is living in every person will not allow it, and until he is taken out of us, we will have to fight the *good fight* of faith daily.

I have found the closer you get to God, the greater sin seems to become magnified in us. Even Paul said at the end of his life, "That Christ Jesus came into the world to save sinners; of whom *I am chief*" (1 Tim. 1:15, KJV, emphasis mine). Our sin in us is only magnified as we get closer to the light of God, and it reveals any darkness in us.

The question remains, How do we cleanse ourselves? By the truth and light of God's word exposing the darkness in us, which can be a humbling process. If God has told us to cleanse ourselves even as we wash with water every day to cleanse our bodies, then certainly He will show us how to cleanse our sin from our lives!

> And have *put on* the new self, *which is being renewed in knowledge* in the image of its Creator. (Col. 3:10, NIV, emphasis mine)

> But *put on* the Lord Jesus Christ, and make no provision for the flesh in regard to its lusts. (Rom. 13:14, NASB, emphasis mine)

We must "put on" or live the "knowledge" of the truth, for the truth will "renew" our minds so that we will know what is right and no longer live to gratify the desires of our sinful nature. *As we "put on" and live the "knowledge" of the "truth," which is the person and "image" of Jesus Christ, we will be walking in His likeness.* Paul said, "The *knowledge of the truth* that *leads to godliness*" (Titus 1:1, NIV, emphasis mine). The knowledge of the truth will always lead us to live a godly life because our mind and spirit will be filled with the life-changing word of God, and it will not permit us to live for the desires of our flesh. The word in us will rebuke and correct us, and if we walk in sin, there will be a continual war going on inside of us to control our lives. Religious traditions have *no* power to control the desires of our sinful nature. They are dead works that might make us feel good for a while, but the truth of the gospel has the *power* to keep us in line and change us!

> Such regulations [religious traditions] indeed have an appearance of wisdom, with their self-imposed worship, their false humility and *their harsh treatment of the body, but they lack any value in restraining sensual indulgence.* (Col. 2:23, NIV, emphasis mine)

We must use the word of God as our sword and put on our entire spiritual armor to war against fleshly gratifications. If we will submit ourselves to God and resist the devil and all his schemes, he must flee from us! The surpassing greatness of God's power is at work in us to destroy all the works of the devil and our fleshly nature.

> *Grace* and *peace* be multiplied unto you *through the knowledge of God*, and of Jesus our Lord. (2 Pet. 1:2, KJV, emphasis mine)

We receive grace and peace through the true "knowledge" of God. Grace is God's strength and power to live a godly life in the midst of a sinful generation. "For *the grace of God has appeared*, bringing salvation to all men, *instructing us to deny ungodliness and worldly desires* and to live sensibly, righteously and godly in the present age" (Titus 2:11–12, NASB, emphasis mine). God has given us everything that we need to live a godly life in this sinful age. For where sin abounds, His *grace/strength* abound more! We must cry out for more grace every day to live upright before Him.

In chapter 1 of 2 Peter, Peter uses the word *knowledge* five times. It means "to become fully acquainted with." In other words, we must "know" God! He wants us to know Him through

His word and Spirit, yet many Christians seek to "know" the ways of the world more than they are using their time to seek God and to know Him more. When we stand before Him, we will be without excuse because He has given us everything that we could ever need to know Him and to live a godly life on earth. "According as his divine power [grace] *hath given unto us all things that pertain unto life and godliness, through the knowledge of him* that hath called us to glory and virtue" (2 Pet. 1:3, KJV, emphasis mine). We must know Him more each day! When we ask to know Him more, we are pleasing the heart of God, and then He will increase us to know Him more and more. "So that you may walk in a manner worthy of the Lord, *to please Him in all respects*, bearing fruit in every good work and *increasing in the knowledge of God*" (Col. 1:10, NASB, emphasis mine).

We must not only be increasing in the *knowledge* of God, but also increasing in the six other virtues that Peter wrote about like *goodness, self-control, perseverance, godliness, brotherly kindness, and love.* For in doing these seven virtues, we will ensure our entrance into the kingdom of God (see 2 Pet. 1:5–7, 11). "*For if these things are yours and are increasing among you*, they keep you from being ineffective and unfruitful *in the knowledge* of our Lord Jesus Christ" (2 Pet. 1:8, NRSV, emphasis mine). In other words, if we want to continually grow in God, we must be practicing these seven virtues and increasing in them for us to attain more of God's knowledge and likeness. Yes, there will be a great price that we will have to pay in denying our flesh so that we might increase in God. But there always has been. It's called "daily dying to self!" Even if we were seeking the riches of the earth, we would have to pay a great price to get them. But we will not be able to keep them for eternity, for seeking earthly riches is like seeking fools gold. "But if anyone does not have them [these seven virtues], *he is nearsighted and blind*, and has forgotten that he has been cleansed from his past sins" (2 Pet. 1:9, NIV, emphasis mine).

> Therefore, brothers and sisters, *be all the more eager to confirm your call and election, for if you do this* [these seven virtues], *you will never stumble.*
>
> Therefore I intend to keep on reminding you of these things, though you know them already *and are established in the truth* that has come to you. (2 Pet. 1:10, 12, NRSV, emphasis mine).

Growing in Christ's Likeness

It is interesting that none of the epistle writers told us to go out and win the world to Jesus! But that as Christians, we are to be growing in holiness (God's character) and into the full likeness of Jesus so that we might be prepared for His coming.

The evangelical church has so imprisoned our thinking about reaching the world for Jesus before we are fully matured that they forgot our real calling as Christians is for us to grow in the full likeness of Jesus, not reaching the world. Jesus and

John the Baptist both grew in spirit before they did the works of their Father.

> And the child grew and became strong; he was filled with wisdom, and the grace of God was upon him.... And Jesus grew in wisdom and stature, and in favor with God and men. (Luke 2:40, 52; NIV)

John the Baptist "*grew and became strong in spirit*, and he lived in the desert until he appeared publicly to Israel" (Luke 1:80, NIV, emphasis mine). As we cleanse ourselves and grow in the knowledge of God, we are growing in spirit until the day of our revealing with Jesus, for we are now hidden in Christ until that day (see Col. 3:3–4). If God has hidden us as He did His Son, why would we seek to reveal ourselves until that day?

For now our calling as a Christian is to grow and mature in spirit first and foremost, and then return with Jesus to rule over the nations. This will take great faith in God and patience on our part to wait on God's timing. But in the end, it will be worth it to have a powerful ministry like Jesus and John had. "*To the end he may stablish [to make firm or secure] your hearts unblameable in holiness* before God, even our Father, *at the coming of our Lord Jesus Christ with all his saints*" (1 Thess. 3:13, KJV, emphasis mine). God wants to prepare and mature us before Jesus comes with all His saints. God will add people into *His* church by His choosing and election and not by our creative evangelistic ideas. Acts 2:47 (emphasis mine) says, "*And the Lord added to the church daily such as should be saved.*" Jesus sent the *apostles* to all nations to make disciples and to teach the people; *He did not send all Christians* to the nations, and unless God has sent us, we had better stay home and grow in the grace and knowledge of our God! *"But grow in grace, and in the knowledge of our Lord* and Saviour Jesus Christ. To him be glory both now and for ever. Amen"* (2 Pet. 3:18, KJV, emphasis mine).

Paul Mueller said he worked with a well-known evangelist named Thomas Wyatt in the early 1950s to the mid-1960s. Paul wrote,

> I respected him highly in the Lord, and learned much from his anointed ministry, especially during the "latter rain" revival of 1948–1953. During those glorious years, I went to West Africa three times, was an associate minister in the church here, and taught in Bible Schools here and in West Africa. Thomas Wyatt had the world's largest religious radio broadcast in the 1950s [Wings of Healing]. He was on the Mutual and ABC radio networks in this country, and also many large, independent radio stations here and in Canada, Mexico, Europe, and in other countries. He had a mailing list of well over a hundred thousand, and a missionary program that, in my opinion, was among the best in the world at that time [Global Frontiers]. But in the early 1960s, a few years after moving his offices from Portland to Los Angeles, Thomas Wyatt became ill and was in the hospital. I had returned from Nigeria and was in Michigan at the time, so I was unable to see him. One of my friends who was a pastor in California then went to see Thomas Wyatt in the hospital. Dr. Wyatt then told my friend, *"All that*

I have done is wood, hay, and stubble." He passed away shortly after that. Of course, Thomas Wyatt's confession surprised my friend.

A person can have a large ministry attracting the attention of the multitudes, but in God's sight it is all nothing but wood, hay, and stubble. And that old order ministry mentality seems to be affecting some of the remnant of the Lord today. Some in this so-called sonship walk seem to spend their time doing nothing more than reading and publishing books and tapes, and doing other religious works. Some delight in running from one meeting to the next under the guise of getting the message out. *But the message is empty and useless if it fails to bring people to greater spiritual maturity.*

When are we going to see that our religious works only make us feel and look like we are doing something good? In truth, we are only feeding our own egos and not adding one thing to the work of the kingdom. *Christianity is not about doing; it's about becoming like Jesus!* Don't be taken prisoner!

OUR GREAT INHERITANCE

> But Christ was faithful as a Son over His house whose
> house [body] we are, "if" we hold fast our confidence
> and the boast *of our hope* [of sonship] firm until the end.

—Hebrews 3:6 (NASB), emphasis mine

As Christians, we look forward to receiving our great inheritance with Jesus, which is for us to take part in the multimember body of Christ. That is, we will become joint heirs, or *joined as one*, with Jesus in His great inheritance that the Father has given Him in possessing all power and authority in heaven and earth. As a natural father would give his matured son a large inheritance, so God has planned to share the eternal inheritance that Jesus has with all His called, chosen, and faithful matured sons. God has given us His great and magnificent promises so that we might become partakers of His divine nature, character, and attributes. "For by these He has granted to us *His precious and magnificent promises*, in order that by *them you might become partakers of the divine nature*, having escaped the corruption that is in the world by lust" (2 Pet. 1:4, NASB, emphasis mine).

As we believe and take hold of God's magnificent promises, we will be changed by the power of His word. The word of God sown in our heart has the power to give us the strength and hope for tomorrow. His word will also guide us in this time of spiritual darkness that we live in like a great light from within by giving us a glimpse of our future with Jesus. The word of hope *in* us will also be as a fortress of truth that will, like a helmet, protect our mind in these times of testing and tribulation. The word of hope *in* us is truth from God on what is to come. Because we have seen and known the truth, we will not want to lose out on what God has shown and promised us. So we must fight on in the good fight of faith!

> For we have become *partakers* of Christ [the body of Christ], "if" we hold fast the beginning of our assurance firm until the end. (Heb. 3:14, NASB, emphasis mine)

Paul tells us in 1 Corinthians 12:12 that the "Christ" is the multimember body of believers. "For as the body is one, and hath many members, and all the members of that one body, being many, are one body: *so also is Christ.*"

The book of Hebrews tells us plainly that we are called to partake or "take part in" the body of Christ *"if"* we hold fast to our faith until the end. "Whose house [body] we are, *if* we hold fast our confidence and the boast of *our hope* firm until the end" (Heb. 3:6). We have been given much understanding in these great promises of our inheritance in Christ's body, like the one in 2 Corinthians 5:1–2: "For we know that if the earthly tent which is *our house is torn down*, we have a building from God, *a house not made with hands, eternal in the heavens.* For indeed in this house we groan, longing to be clothed *with our dwelling [body] from heaven.*" But this will only come about *"if"* we continue in the faith and follow Jesus until the end! We must forsake all that so easily entangles us in the works of the flesh and the spirit of the age. God has given us way too much understanding in the truths of His word and of our future as the sons of God in His kingdom for us to give up now! We are to "endure" to the end—the end of our carnal man that is!

As sons of God, we will receive an inheritance from the Father; as servants of God, we will receive a reward. An *inheritance* is that which a son receives *by virtue of his relationship to the Father.* It is not a gift, it is not earned—it is his by right. "Wherefore thou art *no more a servant, but a son*; and *if a son*, then an *heir* of God through Christ" (Gal. 4:7, KJV, emphasis mine). But what will the sons be heirs of? The kingdom! A son will receive the kingdom of God, which is for us to be sharers in the body of Christ. A son receives *all* things. "He that overcometh *shall inherit all things*; and I will be his God, and *he shall be my son*" (Rev. 21:7, KJV, emphasis mine). All things are in Jesus; He is the Kingdom that we are to seek first. God's "King"-dom reign and rule is now in our heart so that we might obey Him and receive our promised inheritance.

A servant will receive a reward, which is different from and much less than an inheritance. A reward is given to God's servants as something that is given *for service done.* It is not a free gift, as is salvation. Nor is it bestowed because of a right, as an inheritance. It is *earned* by *works*! "For the Son of man shall come in the glory of His Father with His angels; and then He shall *reward every man according to his works*" (Matt. 16:27, KJV, emphasis mine). Men receive salvation from God as a *gift*, *sons* receive from the Father an *inheritance*, and *servants* receive in consideration of their work a *reward*. *Inheritance is given on the basis of relationship*, while rewards are given because of work done. All believers are saved by grace, but rewarded for works. There is great glory and heavenly wealth awaiting those who become profitable servants, fully equipped to serve. As sons we shall truly receive our inheritance, but as servants, we shall in no wise lose our reward.

Can a son be a servant? Jesus, the Pattern Son, declared, "Just as the Son of Man did not come to be served, *but to serve*, and to give His life a ransom for many*" (Matt. 20:28, NASB, emphasis mine). Jesus was a *Son* to His Father, but He also came as a *servant* unto men. *It is the son that serves!* Jesus was and is a Servant-Son.

In Matthew 3:17 (emphasis mine), the Father proclaimed Jesus to be a *Son*: "This is My *beloved Son*, in whom I am well pleased," and is the same Father that also declared Him as being a *servant*. "Behold My *servant*, whom I uphold; mine elect, in whom My soul delights; I have put My Spirit upon Him: He shall bring forth judgment to the Gentiles" (Isa. 42:1, KJV, emphasis mine). This shows us that unmistakably, this "servant" of the Lord is *Jesus*. This is the Son that came into the world to serve, as we must also!

Our Eternal Inheritance

For this reason Christ is the mediator of a new
covenant, *that those who are called may receive the
promised eternal inheritance*—now that he has died as a
ransom to set them free from the sins committed under
the first covenant.

—Hebrews 9:15 (NIV), emphasis mine

Our calling is to possess God's eternal inheritance. This goes far beyond just going to heaven for our reward. That is a free gift to all who repent and receive Jesus as Lord. But God has promised us much more than our minds can comprehend at this time. This eternal inheritance is the fullness of Him that will never fade away. When we first see the inheritance of God with our spiritual understanding, we get excited and have great energy to seek the promises of God. But after a while, our natural man wants to cancel out all that we have seen with the eyes of our spirit as unreal and unattainable. As time goes by, we can become discouraged in our waiting and seeking for it to come to pass in our lifetime because the natural things that we see with our physical eyes seem to be more attainable than spiritual things. Even though we will be tempted to give up on the promises that God has given us, this is also a part of our training for reigning. Hebrews 6:12 (emphasis mine) tells us, "That you may not be sluggish, but *imitators* of those who *through faith* and *patience inherit the promises.*" Because it is through *faith* and *patience* that we will inherit the promises of God, we must not quit until we have received the prize of our high calling. Remember, He is faithful!

> Let us hold fast the confession of our hope without wavering, for *He who promised is faithful.* (Heb. 10:23, NASB, emphasis mine)

> By faith even Sarah herself received ability to conceive, even beyond the proper time of life, since *she considered Him faithful who had promised.* (Heb. 11:11, NASB, emphasis mine)

> *For ye have need of patience,* that, after ye have done the will of God, *ye might receive the promise.* (Heb. 10:36, KJV, emphasis mine)

Our *faith* and *hope* must enter within the veil of the Holy of Holies to be one with Jesus because "*faith* is the *assurance* [freedom from doubt] of things *hoped* for [expected]" (Heb. 11:1, NASB, emphasis mine). Let me make it very clear: we will not enter into the realm of the fullness of God unless we have *faith* and *hope* for this to take place in our life! "This *hope* we have as an anchor [foundation] of the soul, a *hope* both sure and steadfast and *one which enters within the veil, where Jesus has entered* as a forerunner for us, having become a high priest forever according to the order of Melchizedek" (Heb. 6:19–20, NASB, emphasis mine). Our *hope* of entering in with Him into the Holy of Holies must be our anchor and firm foundation of our Christian lives that is rooted and grounded in the promises of God. There is no greater calling or hope in all of life than this high and holy calling. We have not yet entered into this spiritual experience. While we have entered the Outer Court through our salvation experience and experienced the Holy Place through our baptism in the Holy Spirit, we are still waiting for Jesus to reveal Himself in the fullness of His Spirit in us. That we might be one with Him and enter into this great experience of the Holy of Holies in total union with Him as a part of His glorious eternal bride and body to bless all nations.

Jesus has gone before us into the experience of the Holy of Holies. *This is the glory and fullness of God.* He has gone in as the Forerunner, meaning He has gone before us as a guide to show us the way into His glory. In the Father's perfect timing, Jesus will lead us in as we follow Him. The Father has made this promise to us as His children, as an oath or pledge so that He must keep His eternal promise unto us.

> Because God wanted to make the unchanging nature of his *purpose* very clear *to the heirs* of what was *promised*, he confirmed it with *an oath* [a promise yet to be fulfilled]. God did this so that, by two unchangeable things in which it is impossible for God to lie, *we who have fled to take hold of the hope* [the promise of sonship] *offered to us* may be greatly encouraged. (Heb. 6:17–18, NIV, emphasis mine)

God has an eternal *purpose and promise* to fulfill: to make us sons of God, a kingdom of priests after the order of Melchizedek.

"For it was fitting for Him, for whom are all things, and through whom are all things, *in bringing many sons to glory*" (Heb. 2:10, NASB, emphasis mine). The promise of sonship is that the Father will make us into the image and nature of His Son Jesus. "For whom He foreknew, He also predestined to *become conformed to the image of His Son*, that He might be the first-born among many brethren" (Rom. 8:29, NASB, emphasis mine). It is impossible for God to lie. He has already *promised* by an *oath* to bring forth sons in the likeness of Jesus; that is, all who follow the Lamb wherever He goes. This should give us strong hope as we press onward and upward to our heavenly calling. "Faithful is He who calls you [to sonship], and He also will bring it to pass" (1 Thess. 5:24, NASB, emphasis mine).

Paul Mueller wrote the following concerning this holy priesthood:

> God said to Moses, "Ye have seen what I did unto the Egyptians, and how I bare you on eagles' wings, and brought you unto myself. Now therefore, if ye will obey my voice indeed, and keep my covenant, then ye shall be a peculiar treasure unto me above all people: for all the earth is mine: *and ye shall be unto me a kingdom of priests, and an holy nation*" (Exod. 19:3–6, KJV).
>
> *The plan and purpose of God*, to have a holy and anointed people to be to Him *a kingdom of priests* and a holy nation was set forth to Moses and the nation of Israel. And that divine purpose is now being fulfilled. The Lord is now raising up "a kingdom of priests, and an holy nation" to represent Him and His kingdom purposes in

the earth. This wonderful purpose has not changed from the time of Moses to this day. The same divine purpose is repeated several times throughout the scriptures. Isaiah prophesied of a time to come when the Lord would take a people out of Israel: "for priests and for Levites" to administer His affairs in "the new heavens and the new earth" which He declared He would make. (See Isa. 66: 21–22, 61:6, and 2 Pet. 3:10–13). God's purpose to have a kingdom of priests is woven throughout the scriptures as a divine thread of blue, signifying the heavenly reign of holy, anointed, Christ-like kings and priests. (See Ex. 28:3 1, 39:22, Esther 8:15–19). We are that "kingdom of priests." Our Father has born us as on eagle's wings, and brought us unto Himself. We are gathered by the Lord unto Him, not to man. And now, this holy calling unto kingdom priesthood is being fulfilled in the remnant that we are.

Peter also said to the "Elect according to the foreknowledge of God the Father... Ye also, as lively stones, *are built up* a spiritual house, an *holy priesthood*, to offer up spiritual sacrifices, acceptable to God by Jesus Christ" (1 Peter. 1:2, 2:5). This passage indicates that our high calling as a kingdom of priests is a complete and finished work. All we need to do to enter into that realm of kingdom priesthood is to ascend in the Spirit and take our seat in Christ. But we cannot ascend in the Spirit to His throne on our own. Only when Father invites us to "come up hither" can we do so. The book of Revelation also shows that this is already fulfilled in Christ. John has thus declared, "*And hath made us kings and priests unto our God and his Father; to him be glory and* dominion for ever and ever. Amen." — *"And hast made us* unto our God kings and priests: and we shall reign on the earth." — "Blessed and holy is he that hath part in the first resurrection: on such the second death hath no power, *but they shall be priests of God and of Christ,* and shall reign with him a thousand years" (Rev. 1:6, 5:10, 20:6). *Therefore, the original word, given to Moses when he ascended Mount Sinai in Israel's history, is being fulfilled in us in this great day of the dominion of Christ in the earth.*

We are told in Hebrews 7:28 that God has made an *oath* (a promise yet to be fulfilled) to us to bring forth a high priesthood of sons into the earth. "For the Law appoints men as high priests who are weak, *but the word of the oath,* which came after the Law, *appoints a Son,* made perfect [completely mature] forever." The word of *oath* appoints a son completely matured like Jesus to the order of high priest so that they may minister directly unto God (see Ezek. 44:15–16). This "Son" is the multimember body of Jesus that will not be bound by a term or be limited by time to serve as a high priest because they will have been given an indestructible life as Melchizedek and Jesus was. "And this is clearer still, if another priest arises *according to the likeness of Melchizedek,* who has become such not on the basis of a law of physical requirement, *but according to the power of an indestructible life*" (Heb. 7:16, NASB, emphasis mine).

What we are now seeing is just a glimpse of our great inheritance that He has promised unto us *if* we are faithful to serve Him unto the end. "And so *after waiting patiently,* Abraham received what was promised" (Heb. 6:15, NIV, emphasis mine). It is as if God has hidden these marvelous truths from much of the church today because they are unwilling to know and seek Him in His fullness. But if we will seek Him with all our whole heart and not doubt Him, He will reveal Himself to us through the truths of His word and Spirit.

There are many verses in the Bible that speak of our inheritance. I will leave you with a few of these verses from Psalm 37, which we cannot know their full meaning until God chooses to reveal them to us by His Spirit.

> But the humble *will inherit* the land, and will delight themselves in abundant prosperity. (Ps. 37:11, NASB, emphasis mine)

> The LORD knows the days of the blameless; and *their inheritance* will be forever. (Ps. 37:18, NASB, emphasis mine)

> The righteous *will inherit* the land, and dwell in it forever. (Ps. 37:29, NASB, emphasis mine)

> Wait for the LORD, and keep His way, and He will exalt you to *inherit* the land; when the wicked are cut off, you will see it. (Ps. 37:34, NASB, emphasis mine)

CHERUBIM, PROTECTORS OF THE GLORY

> So He drove the man out; and at the east of the garden
> of Eden He stationed the cherubim, and the flaming
> sword which turned every direction, to guard the way to
> the tree of life.
>
> —Genesis 3:24 (NASB)

This verse must be one of the saddest things ever written on paper anywhere. Man was now barred from the very Life of God! Even as I write these words, sadness fills my heart because so few Christians do not desire the Life of God. They are so busy searching for the things of the world and being satisfied with them that they make no time for fellowship with God in their daily lives.

Adam and Eve became so caught up in wanting to be *like* God that they decided to take a shortcut to it by obeying the serpent rather than doing it God's way to eat from the tree of life continually. "For God knows that in the day you eat from it your eyes will be opened, and *you will be like God*, knowing good and evil" (Gen. 3:5, NASB, emphasis mine). Their desire to become *like* God was not their sin, just their method! Our goal as Christians is to become Christlike, who is God, for everything about Him is to be desired!

Jesus said in Matthew 5:48, "Therefore you are to be perfect [mature like God], as your heavenly Father is perfect." The only way for them and us to become *like* God in our character is for us to go through the test of obedience, even as Jesus was tested by Satan in the wilderness and passed! Adam and Eve did not have the moral strength and patience to wait on God and for it to be done His way. If they had waited, God would not have driven them out of the garden, and their close fellowship with God would not have been lost. *Patience* is the test we all must pass if we are going to come into the maturity of God. "But let patience have her perfect work, *that ye may be perfect* [mature like God] and entire, wanting nothing" (James 1:4, KJV, emphasis mine). Adam and Eve must not have had the fullness of God in them since the serpent deceived them with the desire to become like God. I believe that God fully intended to give them His power after their character had been proven through testing and after they had partaken of the tree of life. It is no wonder then why we are to rejoice in our tribulations! These trials are conforming us into His likeness and are preparing us to handle God's power with His patience and character.

> Then the LORD God said, "*Behold, the man has become like one of Us*, knowing good and evil; and now, lest he stretch out his hand, and take also *from the tree of life, and eat, and live forever*. (Gen. 3:22, NASB, emphasis mine)

God placed the tree of life right in the middle of the garden so that it would be the greatest blessing to Adam and Eve. God had them in mind when He planted it there to help them grow into His likeness for He is Life, and they were to partake of His Life on a daily basis. In their eating of the tree of life, they were to grow more and more into His character and likeness. While holiness is the character of God, Adam and Eve greatly lacked this quality because it could only be produced through their testing. Eating of the tree of life would have caused them to live forever in either the sinful state or the righteous state, so God had to block the way to the tree of life by the cherubim.

Notice, God did not have the tree chopped down! Oh no, that would be to chop down "*life*" itself, which is God! If this had happened, we would not be able to partake of eternal life God has promised us in the scriptures. "For God so loved the world, that He gave His only begotten Son, that whoever believes in Him should not perish, *but have eternal life*" (John 3:16, NASB, emphasis mine). Jesus has now become the Tree of Life to all those who would receive Him as Life itself. "For just as the Father has life in Himself, *even so He gave to the Son also to have life in Himself*" (John 5:26, NASB, emphasis mine).

So whatever did happened to the tree of life? Did it die and dry up into dust? Is it still a vibrant tree alive somewhere on planet Earth, but we just haven't found it yet? Or was the paradise of God, the garden of Eden, really another spirit realm in the creation of God, along with the tree of life? I believe the latter to be true because of what Jesus promised us in the book of Revelation regarding this *same* tree of life.

> He that hath an ear, let him hear what the Spirit saith unto the churches; to him that overcometh will *I give to eat of the tree of life*, which is *in the midst [middle of the garden] of the paradise of God*. (Rev. 2:7, KJV, emphasis mine)

> Blessed are they that do his commandments, that they may have right to *the tree of life*, and may enter in through the gates into the city. (Rev. 22:14, KJV, emphasis mine)

These verses teach us that the paradise of God and the tree of life are real because they are of the spirit world and they are eternal. It was not a natural tree that was corrupted by the fall of man or by the curse of God upon the earth. The fruit and seed of this tree still remain for all who will overcome in this life! Paul said in 2 Corinthians 12:2–4 (emphasis mine), "I know a man in Christ who fourteen years ago whether in the body I do not know, or out of the body I do not know, God knows such a man *was caught up to the third heaven*. And I know how such a man whether in the body or apart from the body I do not know, God knows *was caught up into Paradise*, and heard inexpressible words, which a man is not permitted to speak." According to Paul, the paradise of God and the third heaven still remain intact, just as it was created in the beginning.

My belief is that all things will be restored on earth as they were before the fall. We know that the Bible teaches us that there is a second and third heaven. The second heaven is where

Satan is prince over the realm of darkness, and the third heaven is where Jesus is King of kings over all the realms. This leaves us with the first heaven, which we know little of. But it too must be restored to its rightful place during the millennial reign of Christ. Genesis 1:1 (emphasis mine) tells us, "In the beginning God created the *heavens* and the earth." Notice that God created the "heavens," meaning more than one, while He created only one earth. I believe that Adam and Eve were created with a spiritual body much like what Jesus now has in heaven: of dust and a glorified spiritual body at the same time (see Luke 24:39, Phil. 3:21, and 2 Cor. 5:1–2). When Adam and Eve fell into sin, God covered them with natural skin that sweats and stinks as a part of the curse upon them. Having these bodies of *humiliation* rather than bodies of God's glory. "And the LORD God made garments [covers] of skin for Adam and his wife, and clothed [wrapped around] them" (Gen. 3:21, NASB). When they fell into sin, they fell into a lower state or realm of being than what they were first created to be in. Satan was now ruling over them because he was created as a spirit that was now higher than the natural realm. "For our struggle is not against flesh and blood, but against the rulers, against the authorities, against the powers of this dark world and against *the spiritual forces of evil in the heavenly realms*" (Eph. 6:12, NIV, emphasis mine).

The Cherubim

So He drove the man out; and at the east of the garden
of Eden *He stationed the cherubim*, and the flaming
sword which turned every direction, *to guard the way to
the tree of life.*

—Genesis 3:24 (NASB), emphasis mine

Eating of the tree of life after the fall would have caused them to live forever in the sinful state, so God had the tree of life blocked by the cherubim with a flaming sword. The cherubim blocked man's way back to the tree of life, which is the presence and glory of God. Man was now locked out from the eternal Life of God by a flaming sword! I believe that the flaming sword was the power of God's spoken word that blocked the way to life, even as God's word cursed the earth after the fall. "Is not My word like fire?' declares the LORD" (Jer. 23:29, NASB). At God's word, the whole universe came into being, so why would it be so difficult for us to believe that His word of fire would not also prevent us from eternal Life, which is Jesus? It is also interesting to note that the word *sword* and the word *word* only have one letter difference between them—*S*. His word is the sword of the Spirit with which we are to do battle!

Cherubim in the book of Hebrews 9:5 are called "the cherubim of glory." They are angelic beings that were created by God to guard man from coming close to the glory of God. In scripture, they were only spoken of as guarding the way to God's glory. In the book of Exodus, we find them spoken of as *covering* the mercy seat on the ark of the tabernacle, which represents the presence and glory of God.

> And you shall make *two cherubim* of gold, make them of hammered work at the two ends of the mercy seat. And make one cherub at one end and one cherub at the other end; you shall make the cherubim of one piece with the mercy seat at its two ends. And *the cherubim shall have their wings spread upward, covering the mercy seat with their wings* and facing one another; the faces of the cherubim are to be turned toward the mercy seat. (Exod. 25:18–20, NASB, emphasis mine)

In the Tabernacle, man was again barred from the presence of God and of having a personal revelation of who God is. Only the High Priest with the blood of the lamb could go into the Holy of Holies once a year where the ark was to atone for the people's sin that year. He did not go in for his own personal benefit of knowing God more, only for the forgiveness of their sin so that God's presence in the ark would remain with them another year as they camped and traveled to the Promised Land. It was a very dangerous and terribly fearful thing to enter God's glory with sin in their heart. This should stand as a warning to us!

The presence of the cherubim was so complete over the ark that they covered not only the ark of God's presence, but the whole outside of the tabernacle! "Moreover you shall make the tabernacle with ten curtains of fine twisted linen and blue and purple and scarlet material; *you shall make them with cherubim*, the work of a skillful workman" (Exod. 26:1, NASB, emphasis mine). God had Moses make a curtain to cover the tabernacle with the cherubim embroidered in them and in the veil that covered the entrance to the Holy of Holies. "And you shall make a veil of blue and purple and scarlet material and fine twisted linen; *it shall be made with cherubim*, the work of a skillful workman" (Exod. 26:31, NASB, emphasis mine).

According to scholars, there were twenty-three cherubim in all embroidered on the curtain and veil to physically cover and guard the tabernacle of God from man, along with the two covering the mercy seat. I believe that these were just symbolic representatives of what was really there in the spirit world that guarded the presence of God twenty-four hours a day from man.

The fire of God's presence in the Holy of Holies would have killed a person just like a hot light attracts and kills bugs that come too close! Only the blood of Jesus can cleanse us from our sin so that we can come into His presence. The presence and glory of God is what people desire most because that's what they lost in the garden, even though most people don't know that's what they are missing in their life. God had Moses remind the people twice not to come too close to the mountain and gaze at God, or they would be killed. "Then the LORD spoke to Moses, 'Go down, warn the people, lest they break through to the LORD *to gaze*, and many of them perish'" (Exod. 19:21, NASB, emphasis mine). Oh, how much sense this all makes to me now of God's master plan! How awesome! How ingenious is our God that we serve!

Moving Beyond the Cherubim

And behold, the veil of the temple was torn in
two from top to bottom, and the earth shook;
and the rocks were split.

—Matthew 27:51 (NASB)

When Jesus died on the cross, the veil to the Holy of Holies was torn in two, giving man access to *know* God. The cherubim that once blocked the way to God now welcomed man to come in by the blood of the Lamb. I truly believe that these same cherubim that blocked the way in were the same ones that tore the veil in two, gladly opening the way back to God. It has been said that the veil was so thick that two oxen could not have torn the veil in two! "Since therefore, brethren, *we have confidence to enter* the holy place by the blood of Jesus, by a new and living way which *He inaugurated for us through the veil, that is, His flesh*" (Heb. 10:19–20, NASB, emphasis mine). Think about it. We now have access to know the God of creation individually as if we were the only person in the whole universe! God wants to reveal Himself to you and me! "That the God of our Lord Jesus Christ, the Father of glory, *may give to you a spirit of wisdom and of revelation in the knowledge of Him*" (Eph. 1:17, NASB, emphasis mine). Nowhere in the Old Testament were people able to get close to God, but He now dwells in us to reveal Himself in and through us as we await the full revelation of Jesus Christ in us (see 1 Pet. 1:7, 13). How precious we must be to God for Him to allow His presence and glory to come and dwell in us, for we are now vessels of His glory! Wow!

We, as the vessels of God, must partake of Him daily through the tree of Life so that we will grow up into all His likeness. "Beloved, now are we the sons of God, and it doth not yet appear what we shall be: but *we know that, when he shall appear, we shall be like him*; for we shall see him as he is" (1 John 3:2, KJV, emphasis mine). Please hear me clearly, my friend: "We shall be like him," possessors of God's Life eternally, to give away to whom all God wills. Literally, we will have become trees of life even as Jesus is! Don't you see? A tree has seed in its fruit to reproduce after its own kind in the earth! "Truly, truly, I say to you, unless a grain of wheat falls into the earth and dies, it remains by itself alone; but if it dies, *it bears much fruit* [in its likeness]" (John 12:24, NASB, emphasis mine). So now Jesus, the Tree of Life, has reproduced Himself in the earth, with many trees made into His likeness to bring forth healing to the nations from sin and death! How else would there be a tree of life on both sides of the river of life in the New Jerusalem? "In the midst [the tree of life was in the middle] of the street of it, and *on either side of the river, was there the tree of life* [many trees], which bare twelve manner of fruits, and yielded her fruit every month: and *the leaves of the tree were for the healing of the nations*" (Rev. 22:2, KJV, emphasis mine). See also Revelation 22:19. We are likened to trees throughout scripture, so why should it be so hard for us to believe that we become trees of life also? Who will believe the report of the Lord?

And he shall be *like a tree planted* by the rivers of water, that bringeth forth his fruit in his season; his leaf also shall not wither; and whatsoever he doeth shall prosper. (Ps. 1:3, KJV, emphasis mine)

The righteous shall flourish *like the palm tree*: he shall grow like a cedar in Lebanon. Those that be *planted in the house of the* LORD shall flourish in the courts of our God. *They shall still bring forth fruit in old age*; they shall be fat and flourishing. (Ps. 92:12–14, KJV, emphasis mine)

Blessed is the man that trusteth in the LORD, and whose hope the LORD is. *For he shall be as a tree planted by the waters*, and that spreadeth out her roots by the river, and shall not see when heat cometh, but her leaf shall be green; and shall not be careful in the year of drought, neither shall cease from yielding fruit. (Jer. 17:7–8, KJV, emphasis mine)

It will be said, *"Look what the Lord has done, for He has made us oaks of righteousness, the planting of the Lord!"* When I think about what the Lord has done for us, I am awestruck, for He has taken us from being mere worms in the earth and has seated us in the third heaven with Him! For some reason I still believe that the cherubim are still protecting the glory of God in the tabernacle, we being the tabernacle of God! Now we must wait in hope for the full revelation and manifestation of Jesus in and through us. "But if we hope for what we do not see, with perseverance we wait eagerly for it" (Rom. 8:25, NASB).

Unveiling the Glory

*But we all, with unveiled face beholding as in a mirror the
glory of the Lord [Jesus, the Word], are being transformed
into the same image [Jesus, the Word] from glory to glory,*
just as from the Lord, the Spirit.

—2 Corinthians 3:18 (NASB), emphasis mine

Anyone who listens *to the word* but does not do what
it says *is like a man who looks at his face in a mirror* [the
word] and, after looking at himself, goes away and
immediately forgets what he looks like. But the man
who looks intently into the perfect law [the word] that
gives freedom, and continues to do this, not forgetting
what he has heard, but doing it—he will be blessed in
what he does.

—James 1:23–25, (NIV), emphasis mine

Now that the veil has been torn in two and the way has been
opened for us to gaze and wonder at God, now what? We are
now able to receive as much of God as we desire through divine
revelation as we draw close to Him. Jesus is the word and glory
of God; by seeing Him, we grow spiritually and are changed. As
we see the reflection of Jesus Christ in His revealed word, *we are
seeing the glory of the Lord.* We are slowly being changed into His
image and likeness day by day. In order for us to be changed into
His likeness, we must *see* Him in the word by the revelation of

the Spirit of God and by us having intimacy with Him. Also, we hear His anointed word through the spoken and written word and by hearing Him through friends and loved ones. Because the Lord now embodies His people, this is one way He chooses to speak to us. It is an ongoing revelation of Jesus Christ that we must be seeking after if we are going to be changed into His glory. It is from glory level to glory level of His word and Spirit that makes us become more like Him. We did not grow up physically overnight, and we will not be transformed into His glory overnight either. It's an ongoing, line-upon-line, truth-upon-truth revelation of Him that will cause us grow up into His likeness. "But *speaking the truth in love, we are to grow up in all aspects into Him*, who is the head, even Christ" (Eph. 4:15, NASB, emphasis mine). We must begin to see and hear our good Shepherd in those around us in order for us to grow. Very few Christians are able to see and hear Him in others. Those of us who are seeking Him miss Him many times as He speaks to us through people. Why is this? Because of our pride and lack of humility! We must humble ourselves before God and others if we really want to hear Him.

For sometime I had been asking the Lord to reveal to me how I could be filled with all His fullness as we have been promised in scripture "that you may be filled up *to all the fullness of God*" (Eph. 3:19, NASB, emphasis mine). How can a person possibly receive His fullness unless he can see it with his heart? Then one day I saw it in 1 John 3:2 (emphasis mine): "When He shall appear, we shall be like Him; *for we shall see Him as he* is." *It is in seeing Him that makes us like Him!* It is that simple, my friend! For what you behold, you will become like. Now the question remains, how do we see him? Must Jesus come and stand before us in person for us to see Him as He is? No! We must see Him through the revelation of His word and Spirit, which is us having the eyes of our understanding opened to the ways of God and His word and by us having our minds renewed to see the truth of who He is. This will change us into His likeness even now—today we must see Him by the Spirit, even though we still see Him dimly.

> For now we see *in a mirror dimly*, but then *face to face*; now I know [HIM] in part, but then I shall know [HIM] fully just as I also have been fully known. (1 Cor. 13:12, emphasis mine)

God's word promises us that we will not always be looking in a mirror dimly to see Him. For one day we are going to see Him *"face-to-face,"* and not in a poor reflection of who He is, but in a clear revelation when He is revealed in fullness. Revelation always takes place first in our hearts before it goes into our heads! God is slowly giving us a clearer revelation of who He is as we seek His face. "For God, who said, 'Light shall shine out of darkness,' is the One who has shone in our hearts *to give the light of the knowledge of the glory of God in the face of Christ*" (2 Cor. 4:6, emphasis mine). Notice that the light\truth and glory of God is only found *in the face of Jesus*! The face of a person is the revelation or manifestation of what they are and what is going on inside of the person. If a person is sad, glad, or mad, the face of that person will change to reveal what is going on in their heart at that time. I have heard many people say that they have seen the literal face of Jesus. They all have said, "His face and eyes radiate with love and warmth." Why is this? Because that is what the heart of God is! The full revelation of God's love is coming to all those that would seek His face daily.

To be face-to-face with someone speaks of closeness and intimacy. The closer you get to a person's face, the more you can look in their eyes and see their heart. It is also interesting to note that human beings are the only species on earth that I know of that are face-to-face in their sexual relationship. This should speak to us about the closeness that God wants to have with us! Moses, being in the Old Testament, was not able to see the face of God and live. But we who are in Christ can see His face and live because we have died with Christ. It is no longer I who live, but Christ in me! "But He [God] said, *'You cannot see My face*, for no man can see Me and live….Then I will take My hand away and you shall see My back, but *My face shall not be seen'*" (Exod. 33:20, 23; NASB; emphasis mine).

In the New Testament, we are called to seek His face and to know Him, not only by the hearing of the ear, but through the revelation of our heart that can only come through intimacy and knowing God in the secret place of His presence. "*Looking to Jesus* the pioneer and perfecter of our faith" (Heb. 12:2, NRSV, emphasis mine).

The Word and glory of God (Jesus) has already shone in our hearts, even as Moses's face shone with the glory of God. The Hebrew word for *shone* is *qaran*, meaning "to push or gore, to shoot out horns of light." It would be like us looking at the sun without any eye protection. It will cause great pain to our eyes. But so will the word of God because it is the greatest light and will cause great pain to those who live in the deception of religion and in the darkness of the world system. Have you ever come out of a dark room and turned on the light? Pain comes to our natural eyes. So it is with our spiritual eyes when we first see new truths in God's word. The light exposes darkness of sin and false doctrine in us! Peter demonstrated this on the day of Pentecost when the people said to him, "Now when they heard this, they were pierced to the heart" (Acts 2:37). The truth of God's word brought great conviction and pain to the hearts of the people because they were not right before God, and their foundation was being shaken.

If we want to see God's glory as Moses did, we must see it in the word as Moses did in the Law, even though it was a fading glory that he and the children of Israel saw. But the New Testament gospel is not a fading glory; it's an eternal one! "And if what was fading away came with glory [the Law], how much greater is the glory of that which lasts" (2 Cor. 3:11, NIV)! Moses had to keep his face covered because the glory of the Law was fading away. "We are not like Moses, who would put a veil over his face to keep the Israelites from gazing at it while *the radiance was fading away*" (2 Cor. 3:13, NIV, emphasis mine). The glory of the gospel of Jesus Christ will never fade away because it is eternal! Hallelujah! Truly, God's glory has been revealed to us through the gospel of Jesus Christ, for He has already given to us His eternal word and truth (see John 17:22). "Giving thanks to the Father, who has qualified us to share *in the inheritance of the saints in light.* For He delivered us from the domain of darkness, and transferred us to the kingdom of His beloved Son" (Col. 1:12–13, NASB, emphasis mine). The revelation of truth in us is the kingdom of God's light and love!

The fading glory of the Lord was upon the Law when it was engraved in stone tablets that were given to Moses on the mountain. The Law was fading because the gospel was to be written upon our heart, and it was to be an unfading glory! "But if the ministry of death, in *letters engraved on stones, came with glory,* so that the sons of Israel could not look intently at the face of Moses because of the glory of his face, *fading as it was*" (2 Cor. 3:7, NASB, emphasis mine). After Moses received the stone tablets, they were to be placed in the Ark of the Covenant within the Holy of Holies. The glory of the Lord remained upon it there until Israel refused to repent of their sin. The glory of the Lord left the Temple of God in Ezekiel 10:18, and it never returned. But now the eternal unfading glory (Jesus Christ) has appeared in earth to free men from the power of sin, "which is the Law" (see 1 Cor. 15:56). John wrote, "The life appeared [Jesus, the glory]; we have seen it [Him] and testify to it, and we proclaim to you the eternal life [Jesus], which was with the Father and *has appeared to us*" (1 John 1:2, NIV, emphasis mine).

God has now given us His eternal light. *It is His word in us so that we might be and live the truth in this dark world!* Jesus said, "You are the light of the world. A city set on a hill cannot be hidden" (Matt. 5:14). The glory of His truth spoken through us is to be given to the world living in the darkness of sin and lies. "Because of the tender mercy of our God, by which the rising sun will come to us from heaven to shine on those living in darkness and in the shadow of death, to guide our feet into the path of peace" (Luke 1:78–79). Jesus is that great Light in us. We must not hide Him any longer, for He/we are the Light of the world.

The very word of Life that Jesus is, is no longer hidden in a golden box somewhere, *but is in us* (the temple of the Lord) to change us into His likeness, for we are *becoming the word of God*! God created man by His spoken word. And by His word (glory) in us, we will again be conformed into His word (Jesus). Our prayer must be "Lord fill me, 'this earth,' with the glory of the Lord and give me the 'knowledge' of your glory so that I may know you more intimately each day!"

> For *the earth [us] will be filled with the knowledge of the glory of the* LORD, as the waters cover the sea. (Hab. 2:14, NASB, emphasis mine)

The scriptures declare that the whole earth is filled with God's glory, even though it seems to be *hidden* from *most* people. So also is His glory *hidden* in His word and people, yet *most* Christians miss Him! The whole purpose of our life on earth is to come into the full likeness of God's glory (Jesus). If we have not grown into this, we have not come into God's perfect will for our life. We cannot just know God's truth, but we must become it! Amen and amen!

THE SEED LIFE OF JESUS IN YOU

In the beginning was the Word, and the Word was with
God, and the Word was God.

—John 1:1 (NASB)

What was from the beginning, what we have heard,
what we have seen with our eyes, what we beheld and
our hands handled, concerning *the Word of Life* and *the
life was manifested* [revealed], and we have seen and bear
witness and *proclaim to you the eternal life*, which was
with the Father *and was manifested [revealed] to us.*

—1 John 1:1–2 (NASB), emphasis mine

As Christians, we cannot wait to see the face and image of
Jesus Christ in person. Yet the Bible teaches us that the living
Word of God is the image and likeness of Jesus, which has
been revealed *in us*. If we want to know and see Him as He
really is, we do not have to go any farther than receiving the
Life of His Spirit, for He is the Eternal Life, the exact image
and representation of the Father. When the disciples wanted
to see the Father, "Jesus answered: 'Don't you know *me*, Philip,
even after I have been among you such a long time? *Anyone who*

has seen me has seen the Father. How can you say, "Show us the Father"?'" (John 14:9, NIV, emphasis mine). Jesus, the Word, is the exact image and likeness of the Father who we so desire to see and know more clearly, no longer seeing Him through a glass darkly. As we dimly see Him now, this gives *spiritual* Life unto us. But when we see Him face-to-face, it will give Life unto our *mortal bodies*, and we will be changed! "For now we see in a mirror dimly, but then face to face; now I know [Him] in part, but then I shall know [Him] fully just as I also have been fully known" (1 Cor. 13:12, NASB).

There is a spiritual "highway" to "life" in God that we are called to walk on, and it will lead us through a "narrow gate" unto the transformation of our bodies. "Enter through the narrow gate; for the gate is wide [broad] and the road is easy that leads to destruction [loss], and there are many who take it. Because narrow [suffering] is the gate and difficult is the way *which leads to life, and there are few who find it*" (Matt. 7:13–14, NKJV, emphasis mine).

If we walk with the multitudes in this new day, we will find ourselves going through "the wide gate" or "broad way" that leads to "destruction." The word *destruction* in the Greek means "ruin or loss." To walk the broad way of this world is to have the ruin or loss of the precious Life of Christ that would transform us into His glorious image and likeness.

I find it interesting that one of the most famous roads in the entire world is called Broadway! It is a main thoroughfare of New York State and is one of the longest streets in the world. It begins at the southern tip of Manhattan and extends about 150 miles north to Albany, New York. It runs through Times Square in New York City; this is the principle theater and worldly amusement district of the city. As the Broadway of New York City is representative of the world system, so is the broad way or the "easy life" of sin that leads to "ruin or loss" for all those who would travel on it in this life! The narrow gate of suffering and judgment is difficult for us now, but is nothing compared to the suffering of those who walk on the broad way of life now and what they will suffer later in the lake of fire judgment! Do not envy the apparent prosperity of the wicked, for it is only temporary and not true reality. It will all crumble to the ground one day, just as the World Trade Towers did in New York City. But we who live for spiritual realities (truth) will have them throughout eternity! David said in Psalm 73:3–6, 12–19:

> For I was envious at the foolish, when I saw the prosperity of the wicked. For there are no bands in their death: but their strength is firm. They are not in trouble as other men; neither are they plagued like other men. Therefore pride compasseth them about as a chain; violence covereth them as a garment....Behold, these are the ungodly, who prosper in the world; they increase in riches. Verily I have cleansed my heart in vain, and washed my hands in innocency. *For all the day long have I been plagued, and chastened every morning.* If I say, I will speak thus; behold, I should offend against the generation of thy children. When I thought to know this, it was too painful for me; *until I went into the sanctuary of God; then understood I*

their end. Surely thou didst set them in slippery places: *thou castedst them down into destruction.* How are they brought into desolation, as in a moment! They are utterly consumed with terrors.

Our heavenly Father is leading His elect to go through the narrow gate of judgment now in this lifetime. This narrow way leads to the *fullness* of the Life of Christ, which is the transformation of the spirit, soul, and body. Jesus said, "*Narrow* is the gate [doorway] and difficult [suffering] is the way [the roadway] *which leads to [the fullness of] life, and there are few who find [obtain life] it.*" The word *narrow* means "to be hemmed in a tight pass or doorway between the rocks." In other words, as we are climbing spiritual Mount Zion, we find ourselves in difficult places that seem to make it almost impossible for us to travel upward into His *fullness* of Life. Jesus said it would be difficult for us to follow His *way* to the *fullness* of Life. The word *difficult* means "to suffer tribulations and hardship." I believe what Jesus is saying by this is "People are willing to pay the high price of suffering for many things in this natural life, like being rich, having a college education, or to obtain fame. But few will pay the high price of traveling upward this spiritual Mount Zion to obtain the *fullness* of His Life that He has promised to all those who would trust Him for it."

If we will seek Him on the *highway to Life* that He has promised to give us, He will then help us travel on it with the help of His presence. "You have made known to me the paths [roadway] of life; you will fill me with joy in your presence" (Acts

2:28, NIV). Our job is to stay on the path of Life and stay out of the ditch that is on either side of this path. If our desire is to go to the top of Mount Zion and be swallowed up by His Life, then this is a must! Sin, depression, doubt, fear, and unbelief will put us in the ditch and keep us there until we call out to our Shepherd to pull us out by His grace. If we are spending time in the ditch, we are not traveling upward to our high calling of the renewed mind in the likeness of Jesus, and we will delay our transformation into His likeness at the top of Mount Zion. This is not just a given because we have received Jesus into our hearts, but must be obtained through our *enduring unto the end.* "Through *many tribulations* we must enter the kingdom of God [the kingdom of His Life]!" (Acts 14:22, NASB, emphasis mine). Through our suffering and great tribulations, we find the way to enter in; there is just no other way into the *fullness* of His of Life. Paul said we are "always carrying about in the body the dying of Jesus, *that the life of Jesus also may be manifested in our body. For we who live are constantly being delivered over to death for Jesus'* sake, *that the life of Jesus also may be manifested in our mortal flesh*" (2 Cor. 4:210–11, NASB, emphasis mine). If the dying of Jesus is not in our self-life, there cannot be the Life of Jesus manifested through us to others either!

Pressing Forward

We, as the church of Jesus Christ, must move forward in and through this dying process if we are going to obtain His Life. We must stop loving the world and its Babylon religious system of our day and not go back to its ways. Why is it that the church of Jesus Christ as a "movement" has not progressed forward, but has gradually regressed backward to her religious ways? The whole church has not grown spiritually in truth and into the likeness of Jesus, nor has it progressed in all fields as much as the world system did over the last century, especially in the area of knowledge and technology.

This last century, the world has gone forward in almost every field but truth! But soon great advances are in order for the church of Jesus Christ! We are promised in Romans 8:11, "But if the Spirit of Him who raised Jesus from the dead dwells in you, He who raised Christ Jesus from the dead *will also give life [God's Life eternally] to your mortal bodies* through His Spirit who indwells you." These earthly bodies must be changed! Think about it. Everything that naturally comes out of the physical body stinks; they stink inside and out because they are bodies of the sin nature! We must take baths to keep from stinking and then put deodorant on (which means to kill the stink), then on top of that we put on perfume! We brush our teeth and suck on mints to keep from offending others, and I will not write much about the smell that comes out from our stomachs and after we have eaten! But oh, how we will enjoy our glorified bodies made after the likeness of Jesus! They will no longer need any physical makeup to make them look or smell better, for they will have the fragrance and beauty of God Himself! Wow!

> He will transform *the body of our humiliation* that it may be conformed to the body of his glory, by the power that also enables him to make all things subject to himself. (Phil. 3:21, NRSV)

And that's what our physical bodies are, "humiliation" compared to our spiritual bodies in heaven.

God told Daniel about the future end times, that there would be great advances in the earth and in the revealed word of God, depending on what translation you read it in.

> But as for you, Daniel, conceal these words and seal up the book until the end of time; many will go back and forth, and knowledge will increase. (Dan. 12:4, NASB)

The amplified Bible reads this way, which I believe is correct.

> But you, O Daniel, shut up the words and seal the book until the time of end. [Then] many shall run to and fro and search anxiously [through the book], and knowledge [of God's purposes as revealed by His prophets] shall be increase and become great. (Dan. 12:4)

Great knowledge has increased in the earth, both in the revelation of God's word and in the world system to advance their causes in all fields. Yet few Christians have taken advantage of these historic times that we live in to seek God for greater revelations of Himself. Most believers have run toward the world system to become wealthy in earthly riches, having become spiritual adulteresses with the world system of man. "You adulteresses, do you not know that friendship with the world is hostility toward God? Therefore whoever wishes to be a friend of the world makes himself an enemy of God" (James 4:4, NASB). Somehow, many Christians have been deceived to think that receiving the riches of the world was God's real blessing on them and was more important than receiving the true riches of the kingdom that were to be implanted within their heart. It's no wonder that John the revelator calls the church system "the great whore" that controls the minds of many people on the earth (see Rev. 17:1, 15). Many preachers within the church system teach foolishness while the truths of God go unclaimed and undesired by most believers.

Some of the Greeks of Jesus's day had enough sense to seek Him instead of the things of the world.

> Now there were certain Greeks [these were intellectuals] among those who were going up to worship at the feast; these therefore came to Philip, who was from Bethsaida of Galilee, and began to ask him, saying, "Sir, *we wish to see Jesus.*" Philip came and told Andrew; Andrew and Philip came, and they told Jesus. And Jesus answered them, saying [listen to Jesus's answer as He tells them how to see Jesus], "The hour has come for the Son of Man to be glorified [through His death they would see

Him in His full grown body of sons]. Truly, truly, I say to you, unless *a grain of wheat falls into the earth and dies* [Jesus], it remains by itself alone; but if it dies, it bears much fruit [Christ the seed was buried in us to bare fruit in His likeness through us]. He who loves his life loses it; and *he who hates his life in this world shall keep it to life eternal*. If anyone serves Me, *let him follow Me*; and where I am, there shall My servant also be [and where is that? On the throne]; if anyone serves Me, *the Father will honor him* [to sit on my throne]." (John 12:20–26, NASB, emphasis mine)

Jesus said in Matthew 13:30, 37–38 (emphasis mine), "Allow both to grow together [the wicked and good seed] *until the harvest* [of the full-grown sons]; and in the time of the harvest I will say to the reapers, 'First gather up the tares and bind them in bundles to burn them up; but *gather the wheat* [the seed of Jesus that was sown in us] into my barn [the precious produce is the sons of God that have grown into His fullness].'"… And He answered and said, 'The one who sows the good seed is the Son of Man, and the field is the world; and as for the good seed [the full grown harvested seed], *these are the sons of the kingdom*; and the tares are the sons of the evil one [the full grown harvested weed seed that is burned in the fire]."

Be patient, therefore, brethren, *until the coming [presence] of the Lord* [for He comes in and through His sons, His first fruits]. Behold, the farmer [God, John 15:1] waits for the precious produce of the soil [which is His character and fruit in the sons], being patient about it, until it gets the early and late rains. (James 5:7, NASB, emphasis mine)

And another angel came out of the temple, crying out with a loud voice to Him who sat on the cloud, "Put in your sickle and reap, because the hour to reap has come, because the harvest of the earth is ripe [the full grown seed, the sons of God]." And He who sat on the cloud swung His sickle over the earth; and the earth was reaped. (Rev. 14:15–16, NASB)

Simply put, when God's fruit or character is full-grown in and through our lives, we must be harvested! We must not allow our trials and tribulations to hinder our spiritual growth any longer, but allow them to cause us to grow into His likeness quicker. God does not lightly allow these troubles to come upon us without a purpose and plan. Paul said in Romans 5:2–5 (emphasis mine, "By whom also we have access by faith into this grace wherein we stand, and rejoice in hope of the glory of God. And not only so, *but we glory in tribulations also: knowing that tribulation worketh* patience; and patience, experience; and experience, hope: and hope maketh not ashamed; because the love of God is shed abroad in our hearts by the Holy Ghost which is given unto us."

It is easy for us to rejoice in the hope of the glory of God; this is only natural for us to rejoice in that which is exciting and expectant. *Yet we are told to rejoice in our tribulations.* Now that's supernatural! Unless we have a revelation of what tribulation can do for us, we will not make it through the severe tests and trials that will open for us the greater revelations of the Lord, which is His full revealing in and through us. Paul said, "Tribulation worketh patience." In other words, *pressures, trials, and afflictions work in us the willingness to suffer the will of God so that we will be matured like Jesus.* Patience means just that, "the willingness to suffer the will of God." We must let tribulations finish their work in us and not try to escape from them if we expect to grow spiritually into His likeness. "Perseverance [patience] *must finish its work so that you may be mature and complete, not lacking anything*" (James 1:4, NIV, emphasis mine).

Our willingness to *stay under* these trials is what is testing our obedience to our heavenly Father through our most trying of circumstances. "Although He was a Son, He learned obedience from the things which He suffered" (Heb. 5:8, NAS). Our goal should be to be like our heavenly Father. "Therefore you are to be perfect [mature], as your heavenly Father is perfect [mature]" (Matt. 5:48, NAS). My goal as an earthly father is to bring my children up and mature them in heart and mind. Should God have anything less than a goal for *us* to be like *Him*?

But Paul does not stop there. He goes on to say in Romans 5:4, "*Patience* [works] *experience.*" We could say, "Patience, or staying under the trial, brings forth tested character in us." This tested character is "Christlikeness" in our heart and mind. When we have gone through our trials and have learned what God wants us to learn from them, we now have His tested character. We have learned experience from them just as a hardened war veteran would have learned to stay cool under fire! "Now, discipline always seems painful rather than pleasant at the time, *but later it yields the peaceful fruit of righteousness to those who have been trained by it*" (Heb. 12:11, NRSV, emphasis mine). When the Lord has trained us through our tribulations, we will have peace in our heart and mind through any circumstances, and nothing will shake us! Our maturity in God is proven when we are *in peace* under fire.

"*Experience or tested character (works) hope: and hope maketh not ashamed.*" How can tested character bring hope? When we see God's faithfulness to keep and deliver us through all of our circumstances as He has promised us in His word, great hope and peace in our inner man. Once we have learned that we can trust God through anything, we will have a greater hope that He will keep His word to us in our present tribulation. As a Christian, we should have one hope and goal. Paul speaks of this hope often in his writings. This hope is not the rapture, nor is it a mansion in heaven; *it is to know Jesus and be like Him*, which is the hope of glory! These tribulations that we are going through are preparing us to be revealed as the sons of God! "For the anxious longing of the creation waits eagerly for the revealing of the sons of God" (Rom. 8:19, NASB). But this will only take place after we have been tried and tested by God.

Resistance Is Good

Submit therefore to God. *Resist* the devil and he will flee from you.

—James 4:7 (NASB), emphasis mine

But *resist* him, firm in your faith, knowing that the same experiences of suffering are being accomplished by your brethren who are in the world.

—1 Peter 5:9 (NASB), emphasis mine

The word *resist* means "to stand or endure against." Resistance works for our good. The things that hinder us only work to make us stronger, just like a weight lifter pushing against his heavy weights. God allows the devil to work against us to only make us stronger spiritually.

Some years ago, I went down to the altar of a church and raised my hands to the Lord in worship for His wonderful presence. Out of nowhere, I felt someone's hands on mine pushing against me, not to the point of pushing me over, but firm and steady. I opened my eyes to see who was there, and to my amazement, there was no one! I thought that was strange! Little did I know that God was trying to speak to me about what was coming in my life: *resistance* from the enemy. This was only to prepare me and make me stronger for His work in the future.

One day I was seeking the Lord on why I didn't have any desire to do some of my past sins and but still had other sinful desires. For instance, I used to smoke and drink, but I have no desire to do those things anymore. But when it comes to wasting my time on the Internet or TV and other things that pull at the carnal man, I still must fight against them. The Lord showed me James 1:12 (emphasis mine): "Blessed is the man that *endureth* temptation: for when he is tried, he shall receive the crown of life, which the Lord hath promised to them that love him." Notice that temptation is not evil in itself, but it must be endured or suffered long against to make us stronger so that we can pass the test that the Lord has allowed in our life. In fact, the Lord has allowed Satan to test us as He did Job and Peter to see if we have built up any resistance against evil. Do you see that when we resist temptation it only works to make us stronger as if we were a weight lifter in our spirit? As we resist temptation, we become stronger and stronger against it, but as we yield to our sin, we only become weaker and weaker, yielding to it the next time we are eventually tempted and are overcome by it. Some people say, "I just could not help myself!" Why is this? Because they have not built up any resistance against that certain temptation. "By what a man is overcome, by this he is enslaved" (2 Pet. 2:19, NASB).

When I first quit smoking, it was very difficult for me because all my old friends smoked, and they tempted me with starting back up again. But after a while, I built up a resistance against it so much that I ended up thinking that smoking was the dumbest thing that I ever did for my health. We definitely suffer against many temptations every day; some we give in to more easily than others because we have not gained any resistance against it and because we still may love our sin to much too part with it. We must ask the Lord to give us a perfect hatred toward all sin before we are overcome by it. "I hate them [sin] with perfect hatred: I count them mine enemies" (Ps. 139:22, KJV).

We must drink the cup of testing. This includes suffering against temptation if we are going to be an overcomer with Jesus. Do you not know that Jesus also suffered temptation in the garden of Gethsemane, the sin of wanting to quit on His way to the cross? He said to Peter, "Put the sword into the sheath; the cup which the Father has given Me, *shall I not drink it*" (John 18:11, NASB, emphasis mine). Yes, we too will suffer through our times of temptation, but He has given us many great promises to deliver us. One of these is found in John 16:33: "These things I have spoken to you, that in Me you may have peace. In the world you have tribulation, but take courage; I have overcome the world."

THIS IS THE DAY OF THE LORD

For this is the day of the Lord GOD of hosts, a day of
vengeance, that he may avenge him of his adversaries
[the man of sin]: and the sword [the Word] shall
devour, and it shall be satiate and made drunk with
their blood [life]: for the Lord GOD of hosts hath a
sacrifice in the north country *by the river Euphrates*.

—Jeremiah 46:10 (KJV), emphasis mine

The sword of the Lord has now been unsheathed to devour
His enemy! This is the day of vengeance on His adversary where
His sword will devour him at the Euphrates. The Euphrates River
represents the carnal mind of man that the sword (Word) of the
Lord will devour. I quote from my book *Revelation, Revealed*:

> And the sixth angel poured out his bowl upon the great
> river, the Euphrates; and its water was dried up, that the
> way might be prepared for the kings from the east. (Rev.
> 16:12, NASB)
>
> Notice that this is also the sixth angel dealing with
> the Euphrates River. Six is the number of man, and the
> difference between man and all of God's other creation is
> that man has been given a will to obey or rebel. Obedience
> can only be learned through obeying God in times of

great suffering (see Heb. 5:8). Very few people ever learn true obedience to God in this lifetime, because of the rebellion in the heart of man against God. (The man of sin in us) must be done away with, and this can only be done by the power of God's spoken Word in His timing.

The Euphrates River in the Old Testament was known as "the great river" (see Gen. 15:18; Josh. 1:4). It flowed through historical Babylon and was the life-blood of the city. Rivers are the life force to many cities even today. Spiritually speaking, as an unsaved person we have one river flowing through us, our spiritual head waters, the Euphrates; (*the great head or stream of reasoning and philosophies of men*). It has become the channel of the strength and wealth of spiritual Babylon (confusion) in the earth. Even as the rivers of the earth have become polluted, so has the mind of man. But when we are saved, we have two rivers flowing through us, the Euphrates (the natural reasoning and understanding and the river of life). This is why Jesus said in John 7:38, "He who believes in Me, as the Scripture said, from his innermost being shall flow rivers of living water." When that which flows out of us is bringing death to the people around us, we can be certain that it is not the river of life. If you attend a church service and you leave feeling worse than when you came, you can be certain that the river of life was not flowing there for you.

In Jeremiah chapter 13, Jeremiah was call by God to go to the Euphrates River and hid a waistband there. Now the question is, why would God have Jeremiah go at least three hundred miles away from his home to hid the waistband in this river, when he could have easily hidden it in the Jordan River that was only a few miles away? There is usually a great lesson to be learned in not only the words that God speaks, but also the places of the stories or visions that God gives.

As Jeremiah was obedient to the Lord and hid the waistband in the Euphrates, he was also instructed to go back after many days and retrieve it. He found that the waistband was totally ruined and worthless. "Then the word of the LORD came to me, saying, "Thus says the LORD, 'Just so will I destroy the pride of Judah and the great pride of Jerusalem. This wicked people, who refuse to listen to My words, who walk in the stubbornness of their hearts (minds) and have gone after other gods to serve them and to bow down to them, let them be just like this waistband, which is totally worthless. 'For as the waistband clings to the waist of a man, so I made the whole household of Israel and the whole household of Judah cling to Me,' declares the LORD, 'that they might be for Me a people, for renown, for praise, and for glory; but they did not listen." (Jeremiah 13:8–11, NASB)

We must understand that the Euphrates River is what caused the waistband to become worthless. It was not the Jordan River or the Tigris River that ruined it, but the Euphrates! God has made us to cling closely to Him in intimacy, but the pride, rebellion, and reasoning of man (the man of sin) causes this relationship with God to be ruined. If we as Christians yield to this Euphrates River in us, we too will backside into the ways of the world that we came from. But if we yield to God and have intimacy with Him we are promised by God, *"That they might be for Me a people, for renown, for praise, and for glory."*

My greatest desire is to have the fullness of God flowing through me, as Paul spoke of in Ephesians 3:19, "And to know the love of Christ which surpasses knowledge, *that you may be filled up to all the fullness of God.*" But in order for this to happen, this Euphrates River in us must be dried up, so that the warring of the flesh and Spirit may stop. Then there will no longer be any mixture of light and darkness in us. As Revelation 16:12 said "Then the King (Jesus) of the east may come (not kings)." He comes from the east (meaning a new day) and will reveal Himself in and through His people in the power and glory of His kingdom flowing through us. This river of life flows from God's throne that is in us. Revelation 22:1 says, "And he showed me a river of the water of life, clear as crystal, (no mixture) coming from the throne of God and of the Lamb." God's throne is in us, for He dwells in us. We are His temple. "And there shall no longer be any curse; and the throne of God and of the Lamb *shall be in it*, and His bond-servants shall serve Him" (Revelation 22:3). "The LORD is in His holy temple; the Lord's throne is in heaven (spirit)…" (Psalms 11:4). His throne and living waters will be *in us*, the New Jerusalem. Hallelujah!

Now the question is, "How will this Euphrates River (our own reasoning) be dried up?" The answer, a drought! What you water grows and what you don't dies. It's that easy! The more obedient we are to God, the more the Euphrates River dries up in us (our own reasoning). But the opposite is true also. The more we disobey, the more strength we give to our own reasoning and in the end we turn away from the things of God. This is why God has been dealing strongly with our obedience over the last few years. He has been having us do things that we would never choose to do in our natural understanding. But in obedience to Him we have obeyed. And what a fire it has been! Yet He has worked out things miraculously for us. *This is to teach us that our own reasoning will cause us to miss the perfect will of God and the farther on we follow the Lord the more difficult it will be on our flesh.* These fiery trials are burning out of us that which is not of God. When a fire is burning it must have fuel to make the fire continue to burn; but once the fuel is gone the fire goes out. When God lifts the fiery trial from our life, it is because the fires have burned away from us the things that were not of Him!

We must understand that this great river of human reasoning is what has got us in the mess we are in since Adam and Eve sinned against God. And in order for us to be restored to the fullness of God, our heart and head must agree together and have no more conflict within us. This brings great tribulation inside of our being along with the pressures and trials of everyday life. Think about it, what society has ever had to face the great temptations and pressures of our day? Satan is working over time on each of God's children to try and cause them to fall into sin and God is allowing these things to test us with fire. But God is using these great tribulations to cleanse us and prepare us to stand before Him in great glory. As we are in these fires we must rejoice, they are our friends!"

"And I said unto him, Sir, thou knowest. And he said to me, These are they which *came out of great tribulation*, and have washed their robes, and made them white in the blood of the Lamb. *Therefore* are they before the throne of God, and serve him day and night in his temple: and he that sitteth on the throne shall dwell among them." (Rev. 7:14–15, KJV)

We must clearly understand prophetically what the Day of the Lord is and who is the enemy of the Lord. Many in the church system believe that the "man" Antichrist and all the people with him are God's enemies. They believe once they are killed in the great tribulation, the world will live in a utopia with Jesus being the supreme leader. But is this really true?

Israel had the same thought pattern the church has today when they said, "If we could be free from the Roman government, then we would be a free people." But was that true? Absolutely not! Israel's problem was not their foreign enemy, for God could deal with them. But their enemy was from within! If they would have been freed from Romans, they would have only been in bondage to another oppressive government shortly after because this was Israel's history, a cycle of freedom and bondage because they would not stop sinning against God. Sin within was Israel's real enemy, and Jesus knew this. This was the purpose for which He came, to set them and the world free from the power of sin! "It was for freedom that Christ set us free; therefore keep standing firm and do not be subject again to a yoke of slavery" (Gal. 5:1, NASB).

Here we are at the end of the age, still fighting the same foe Israel did, the enemy within. But at this time, *the sword shall devour His adversaries!* This sword is the Word of God that will defeat our foe from within. "The LORD says to my Lord:

'Sit at My right hand, *until I make Thine enemies a footstool for Thy feet.*' The LORD will stretch forth Thy strong scepter from Zion [the church], *saying*, 'Rule in the midst of Thine enemies'" (Ps. 110:1–2, NASB, emphasis mine). Great power and revelatory truth in the Word of God is going to be released in His people to defeat this enemy within! God saying, *"Rule in the midst of Thine enemies"* will have than come to pass. Our enemy, the man of sin, will be put under our feet by the revelation of God's Word and Spirit. There will no longer be the fighting of the flesh against the Spirit. The victory will have been won as in Revelation 12:10: "And I heard a loud voice in heaven, saying, *'Now the salvation, and the power, and the kingdom of our God and the authority of His Christ have come.'"*

Notice the words "Now the salvation have come!" I thought we already had salvation? We do, but this is talking about great deliverance power coming forth to set mankind free from the power of the man of sin living inside of each person, bringing restoration to the world. Peter and the writer of Hebrews wrote about this *full* salvation.

> Who are protected by the power of God through faith *for a salvation ready to be revealed in the last time.* (1 Pet 1:5, NASB, emphasis mine)

> So Christ also, having been offered once to bear the sins of many, *shall appear a second time for salvation* without reference to sin, to those who eagerly await Him. (Heb. 9:28, NASB, emphasis mine)

This time, His power is going to be revealed through His body, the church, in a way that the world has never seen. Peter spoke of this on the day of Pentecost when he said,

> "AND IT SHALL BE IN THE LAST DAYS," God says, "THAT I WILL POUR FORTH OF MY SPIRIT UPON ALL MANKIND; AND YOUR SONS AND YOUR DAUGHTERS SHALL PROPHESY, AND YOUR YOUNG MEN SHALL SEE VISIONS, AND YOUR OLD MEN SHALL DREAM DREAMS; EVEN UPON MY BONDSLAVES, BOTH MEN AND WOMEN, I WILL IN THOSE DAYS POUR FORTH OF MY SPIRIT And they shall prophesy. AND I WILL GRANT WONDERS IN THE SKY ABOVE, AND SIGNS ON THE EARTH BENEATH, BLOOD, AND FIRE, AND VAPOR OF SMOKE. THE SUN SHALL BE TURNED INTO DARKNESS, AND THE MOON INTO BLOOD, *BEFORE THE GREAT AND GLORIOUS DAY OF THE* Lord *SHALL COME.* AND IT SHALL BE, THAT EVERYONE WHO CALLS ON THE NAME OF THE Lord SHALL BE SAVED." (Acts 2:17–21, NASB, emphasis mine)

The power of the Holy Spirit is going to be poured out in such a way on this great Day of the Lord that the revelation of truth will be given to all nations to see Jesus for Who He is. Then they will repent of their sin. Great signs and wonders shall be seen with fire, blood, and vapor of smoke. *"And it shall be, that everyone who calls on the name of the Lord shall be saved!"* Many will turn to the Lord through these powerful ministries and manifestations that the Lord is going to release upon the earth.

> On this mountain [of truth] the LORD Almighty will prepare a feast of rich food [truth] for all peoples, a banquet of aged wine—the best of meats [the word] and the finest of wines [His Spirit]. On this mountain [of truth] he will destroy the shroud that enfolds all peoples [the darkness blinding them], the sheet that covers all nations. (Isa. 25:6–7, NIV, emphasis mine)

There is soon coming a day when God will rip this veil of darkness that is covering all nations from seeing the light of the glory of God. Then they will mourn because they were living in His glory at all times without knowing it, yet they did not seek Him or know Him. "Look, he is coming with the clouds [His saints], and *every eye will see him* [spiritual eye], even those who pierced him; and *all the peoples* of the earth will mourn because of him. So shall it be! Amen" (Rev. 1:7, NIV, emphasis mine).

The Day

For at least six thousand years, we have been living with day and night on the earth. As it is in the natural, so it is in the spirit realm—first the natural, then the spiritual. On the earth there is both light and darkness at the same time. One place it is day, and another place it is night. That's just how it is in the spirit world on the earth. We live between light and darkness at all times in the spirit. It's literally living between heaven and hell on earth at the same time. We can choose every day which world we will live in by our emotional reactions to each new day. If we choose to live in Satan's lies, we will live on the dark side of life. We will live in depression, fear, unrest, and bitterness for this is what Satan's domain is. But if we choose to walk in the light, even as He *is* the Light, we will have the peace and joy of God. First John 1:7 says, "But if we walk in the light, as He Himself is in the light, we have fellowship with one another, and the blood of Jesus His Son cleanses us from all sin."

The Day of the Lord is coming at a time when we think not and in a way we think not. It comes as a thief hidden from the view of the undiscerning. We must be ready to receive Him at all times "for you yourselves know full well that the day of the Lord will come just like a thief in the night" (1 Thess. 5:2). "We must work the works of Him who sent Me, as long as it is day; night is coming, when no man can work" (John 9:4, NASB). The day/light/truth is coming at the darkest hour of mankind when no man can work, but when God can work *through us*! "Arise, shine; for your light has come, and the glory of the LORD has risen upon you. For behold, darkness will cover the earth, and deep darkness the peoples; but the LORD will rise upon you, and His glory will appear upon you" (Isa. 60:1–2, NASB). The Day of the Lord is just what it says—*a day*! The "day-light" will come in the midst of the greatest darkness the earth has ever known.

However, the Day of the Lord is going to be darkness for the disobedient people. "Alas, you who are longing for the day of the LORD, for what purpose will the day of the LORD be to you? It will be darkness and not light" (Amos 5:18). But it will be a day of light for the faithful people of God. "Blow a trumpet in Zion, and sound an alarm on My holy mountain! Let all the inhabitants of the land tremble, for the day of the LORD is coming; surely it is near, a day of darkness and gloom, a day of clouds and thick darkness. *As the dawn [sunlight] is spread over the mountains, so there is a great and mighty people;* there has never been anything like it, nor will there be again after it to the years of many generations" (Joel 2:1, NASB, emphasis mine). Paul tells us in Romans 13:12 that the time for living in sin is over and the day is near. "The night is almost gone, and the day is at hand. Let us therefore lay aside the deeds of darkness and put on the armor of light." We must press forward into the light of God's Word. When everything else in the world fails us, we will find that "Thy word is a lamp to my feet, and a light to my path" (Ps. 119:105, NASB). Amen!

In Matthew chapter 13, Jesus teaches about the wheat and the tares being sown in the church. They were both sown into a field, and the man that owned it told the workers to let them grow together until the harvest, then they would be separated. We are coming to a time when all that is sown shall be reaped, whether good or bad. All that is evil shall become as dark as Satan himself. All that is good shall become as Jesus.

In Revelation 14:14–20, two ripened harvests are on the earth, one good harvest for His keeping and one wicked harvest for His wrath. Jesus reaps the good harvest first, then has the angels reap the wicked harvest into the great winepress of the wrath of God. We are now at the end of the age, and the harvests are ripe. *Which harvest will you be of?* Let us turn to God with all our heart and hate evil with a perfect hatred the way God does. For because of this evil, the wrath of God will come. Let us flee from it!

> *But the day of the Lord will come like a thief,* in which the heavens [the mind] will pass away with a roar [sudden crash] and the elements [ways of the world] will be destroyed with intense heat [His presence], and the earth [fleshly body] and its works will be burned up. Since all these things are to be destroyed in this way, what sort of people ought you to be in holy conduct and godliness, looking for and hastening the coming of the day of God, on account of which the heavens [the mind] will be destroyed by burning [His presence], and the elements will melt with intense heat! But according to His promise we are looking for new heavens [the mind] and a new earth [glorified body], in which righteousness dwells. Therefore, beloved, since you look for these things, be diligent to be found by Him in peace, spotless and blameless. (2 Pet. 3:10–14, NASB, emphasis mine)

Again, we are clearly warned in scripture that the Day of the Lord will come like a thief in the night, "for you yourselves know full well that the day of the Lord will come just like a thief in the night….But you, brethren, are not in darkness, that the day should overtake you like a thief" (1 Thess. 5:2, 4; NASB). Jesus is coming unannounced and quietly as a thief to a people that are both prepared and unprepared in their heart. We don't have to be caught off guard if we will seek Him in the beauty of holiness through all our testings and fires before He comes. The problems we are all facing are not of our own making, but from God who is deliberately setting up our path for us to follow Him in. He is preparing our hearts for His revealing "that the proof of your faith, being more precious than gold which is perishable, even though tested by fire, may be found to result in praise and glory and honor *at the revelation of Jesus Christ*" (1 Pet. 1:7, NASB, emphasis mine).

Paul said that two things must take place in order for Jesus to manifest Himself or the Day of the Lord to be revealed: (1) the apostasy or falling away from the faith comes first, and (2) the man of sin is revealed.

> That you may not be quickly shaken from your composure or be disturbed either by a spirit or a message or a letter as if from us, to the effect *that the day of the Lord [the manifestation of Jesus] has come.* Let no one in any way deceive you, for it will not come unless *the apostasy comes first, and the man of lawlessness [man of sin] is revealed, the son of destruction [loss].* (2 Thess. 2:2–3, NASB, emphasis mine)

Both of these things have already come to pass! The church around the world has fallen away from the love and truth of the Lord Jesus and is more like the world than it is like Jesus! The man of sin has been revealed to the elect of God as the *man of sin* that is living inside of every human being. The Day of the Lord is come. The day of *full* revelation of Truth (Jesus) is coming ever clearer until He fully manifests Himself as the Word of God in truth through His elect people with power to save and deliver mankind.

Let us look up; the day of our full redemption (the adoption/placing of sons) has come!

> And not only this, but also we ourselves, having the first fruits of the Spirit, even we ourselves groan within ourselves, *waiting eagerly for our adoption as sons, the redemption of our body.* (Rom. 8:23, NASB, emphasis mine)

Hope for a New Day Arises

God has not left us without a witness of this new day of truth and righteousness arising in the earth, both spiritually and physically. He has given us the hope of the morning star or known as the day star. The morning star is a star of hope, hope for a new day. Years ago when there were no clocks or ways of telling time, at night there was the morning star that gave hope to people that were sitting in the darkness. The morning star really is the planet Venus, coming up every morning about one and a half hour before sunrise. It was a way of telling the people of the earth that a new day was about to begin and the long night is about over.

Jesus said that He Himself was the Morning Star: "I am the root and the offspring of David, the bright morning star" (Rev. 22:16, NASB). In other words, He is the hope of a new day of righteousness and truth arising in the earth for those who are sitting in spiritual darkness. "Because of the tender mercy of our God, with which *the sunrise* from on high shall visit us, *to shine upon those who sit in darkness* and the shadow of death, to guide our feet into the way of peace" (Luke 1:78–79, NASB, emphasis mine). Our God is the God of hope and peace!

Jesus said, "And I will give him [the overcomer] the morning star" (Rev. 2:28, NASB).

Not only is Jesus the bright Morning Star that breaks through the darkness of night, He also promises to give us the morning star in our heart if we will overcome all He has allowed in our lives to test our faithfulness to Him. "And we have the word of the prophets made more certain, and you will do well to pay attention to it, as to a light shining in a dark place, *until the day dawns and the morning star rises in your hearts*" (2 Pet. 1:19, NIV, emphasis mine). Yes, the scriptures are a light in spiritual darkness, but the light of Jesus [the morning star] must be in our heart to give us hope for a new day! "*Until* the day dawns and the morning star *rises in your hearts.*" *The rising of the morning star in our heart is the beginning light and sign of hope for a new day.* Does the hope of the morning star shine within your heart today? Or does the darkness of the night still overshadow you with fears, worries, and the problems of the earth? If you can see the light of this new day arising within you, you have been given the morning star! Hallelujah!

Soon after the morning star rises, it fades away with the brightness of the sunrise of the new day. The lesser light gives way to the greater light. So will it be with us as we have been given *truth* (which is the morning star) to give us hope for a new day in the earth. Then the full brightness and revelation of *truth* that is Jesus will come within our hearts to be manifested through our lives, and we will be like Him! "Then *the righteous will shine forth as the sun* in the kingdom of their Father. He who has ears, let him hear" (Matt. 13:43, NASB, emphasis mine). We not only are called to bear the truth of the morning star now, but we will shine as the sun in its full strength with all its glory and power in truth and righteousness! "But the path of the righteous is like the light of dawn, *that shines brighter and brighter until the full day*" (Prov. 4:18, NASB, emphasis mine). *We are now awaiting our full transformation and manifestation, which will begin the morning sunrise of the "Day" of the Lord through His chosen ones. This will be the complete fullness of the Christ body shining as the sun to bring forth the unadulterated truth of God to the earth!* The sons of God then will set mankind free from the lies and deceptions of the devil and carnal mind (see Rom. 8:21).

> *And those who have insight will shine brightly like the brightness of the expanse of heaven,* and those who lead the many to righteousness, like the stars [sun] forever and ever. (Dan. 12:3, NASB, emphasis mine)

In the morning, the sun does not come up all at once, but comes up gradually until there is "the full day" of sunlight upon the earth. Just as the natural sunlight grows brighter and brighter, His glory becomes brighter and brighter in His people until "the full day." "His radiance is like the sunlight" (Hab. 3:4). His glory will be seen by all nations as His glorious truth comes through His people. "But indeed, as I live, all the earth will be filled with the glory of the LORD" (Num. 14:21, NASB). We are living in such a day!

A LAMB ON THE THRONE

> Then I saw standing there with the throne and the four
> living beings, in the circle of the elders, a Lamb that
> appeared to have been slaughtered. He had seven horns
> and seven eyes, which are the sevenfold Spirit of God
> sent out into all the earth.
>
> —Revelation 5:6 (cjb)

According to this verse, taken literally, a slain Lamb is on the throne. This is truly some strange verbiage here, but we must remember that the book of Revelation is written in a symbolic language (see Rev. 1:1 [kjv]). In reality there is no dead lamb upon God's throne, although there is the living Lamb that paid the price for us to sit with Him upon His throne (see Rev. 3:21). If we truly believe that a slain lamb literally sits on the throne, then we must believe that the Lamb has seven horns with seven eyes coming out of His head. How absurd would it be to believe in such things? No, these are all profound spiritual symbols that the Lord is wanting us to understand with the help of the Holy Spirit. The seven horns are His complete power and authority upon the throne of God, just as His eyes are all seeing and knowing. So also the Holy Spirit is the sevenfold Spirit of God or the completeness of God that is sent into all the earth, which includes you and me and all living things. So clearly we have the triune God represented on the throne and in the earth.

A Lamb of God

A lamb was the first blood sacrifice given by God to cover the sin of man, and without the blood there is no other covering for the sin of mankind. "Abel also brought a gift—the best of the firstborn lambs from his flock. The Lord accepted Abel and his gift, but he did not accept Cain and his gift. This made Cain very angry, and he looked dejected" (Gen. 4:4–5, NLT). With Cain's sacrifice, he did not offer up the blood of the lamb to cover his sin; thus, his sacrifice was not received by God. This made Cain angry enough to kill his brother because he was jealous of his favorable position with God. Rather than Cain going back to sacrifice to God the correct way with a lamb, he chose to sacrifice his brother's blood to repay or atone for his own anger than to do it God's way. However, this was not the right time for a human sacrifice that would one day take away the sin of the world; this would not come for thousands of years until the perfect sinless Son of God would be born. Thank God for that, otherwise we would still be sacrificing lambs!

But because Cain would not do it God's way, he left the presence of God just as his parents Adam and Eve had done. "Then Cain went out from the presence of the Lord, and settled in the land of Nod, east of Eden" (Gen. 4:16, NASU). It is the blood of the lamb that enables us to be drawn near to the heart of God for it was this way since Adam and Eve sinned. We cannot be 100 percent sure what kind of animal skin God used to cover Adam and Eve because the Bible does not say. But from all the other foreshadowings of lambs throughout the Bible, we can be quite sure that it was a lamb that God Himself first sacrificed so that they could live in some form of relationship with God. Abel must have learned to sacrifice lambs from his father in order for him to do this to have a close living fellowship with God.

But it was Isaac that first asked the question, "Where is the lamb?" (see Gen. 22:7). Not knowing of course that he, Isaac, would be the first symbolic human being to become the first lamb to be symbolically sacrificed for the sin of another man. Although it was John the Baptist who first saw a man as the Lamb, Jesus Christ, the first and last human lamb to ever be sacrificed for the sin of man. John proclaimed, "Behold, the Lamb of God who takes away the sin of the world!" (John 1:29, NASU). John knew that the spotless, sinless Lamb had now come so that God could wash man's heart clean of sin with His blood and then fill our heart with His Holy Spirit as He did Adam and Eve in the beginning. And just think, it all came down to the life of a little innocent lamb.

Think of all the millions of little lambs that were sacrificed when God first instituted the Passover lamb in Egypt. God chose this little innocent creature to carry the burden of our forgiveness through its blood and death so that we could draw nearer to the heart of God. The blood was not for God's satisfaction, but so that we could draw near to God without our sin killing us in the process. The question I have for myself is, how am I doing in my sacrifice of self so that others may know and learn of Jesus's great sacrifice for them? Is that not what happens when we choose to sacrifice our will and reputation by telling others about His love for them?

Just as Isaac was a symbolic sacrificial lamb for others, so are we who are called to sit on the throne with Jesus. The throne of God is the mercy seat of God where the Shekinah glory dwelt upon the tabernacle of Moses. That is why there is a slain Lamb upon the throne because lamb's blood was sprinkled upon the mercy seat so that man could come into the presence of God and not be killed. Now the blood of Jesus has been applied to our heart so that God has taken up residence in us, which makes our heart the mercy seat, the throne of God in the earth. How amazing is that?

Our daily life becomes a living sacrifice that is pleasing unto the Father (see Rom. 12:1). Just like Isaac, we have done nothing to deserve to be there but by the destiny of God to glorify His Son's atonement. Each day that we chose to be a living sacrifice of our own will, for the Father's will, we are like a lamb that is being sacrificed, and this is very pleasing to the Lord when we lay down our life for others to gain His life. "We know love by this, He laid down His life for us; and we ought to lay down our lives for the brethren" (1 John 3:16–17, NASU).

This is what we are called to do as sacrificial lambs, to lay our lives down, to learn from Jesus and lay our lives down for our brethren. This is true love and holiness in the sight of the Father, this is the work of the cross, and this is what it means to sit on the throne as a slain lamb. This is death to self, to speak the truth of Who Jesus really is! This is one of the hardest things for us to do, to tell others about Jesus because we do not want to lose face before others and be known as a fanatic. We must sacrifice our reputation as Jesus did if we too are to be like the Lamb of God and sit on His throne.

This is why there is a symbolic slain Lamb upon the throne because His blood washes away all our sin forever so that we also can be a lamb upon the throne with Him, having taken on the nature of the Lamb. For even as He is, so are we; if He is a lamb, so are we, but He is the only one Who died for the sin of the world. Just as Jesus is a Son, so are we! "Beloved, now are we the sons of God, and it doth not yet appear what we shall be: but we know that, when he shall appear, we shall be like him; for we shall see him as he is" (1 John 3:2, KJV). Through the power of the cross, we can forgive the sins of any person that will come to Christ through our testifying to them. This is the work of a slain lamb, not living for themselves (see John 20:23).

To Him Who Sits on the Throne and to the Lamb

> And I saw, and lo, a Lamb having stood upon the
> mount Sion, and with him an hundred forty-four
> thousands, having the name of his Father written upon
> their foreheads. (Rev. 14:1, YLT)

As we read this verse, we see a lamb standing upon Mount Zion, which is the place of the symbolic throne of King David. The 144,000 with the Lamb is a symbolic number of those who are overcomers, which are the sons of God, the bride of Christ, the city of God, the temple of God, and there are many more titles we could use for the overcoming church. These are those who have taken on the nature of the Lamb having His name or His nature written in their minds. In this verse, they have no other titles given to them other than being lambs, with the Lamb of God, because they have become one in nature with the Lamb of God having sacrificed all that they are for His glory alone.

The word *throne* is used forty-two times in the book of Revelation. It is one of the main factors in the book that God wants us to gain an understanding in. He wants us to realize that those who are in Christ have this high calling, that we can have our seat in Jesus, having all that He is upon the throne of authority. As Jesus is the Lamb upon His throne, so are we His people with Him having His name and the likeness of the Lamb of God. We have the seven spirits of God, which is the Holy Spirit, and the seven horns, which is His complete power and authority over all, and having His eyes that are all-seeing and knowing. This is the power of the Lamb upon His throne. It may not now seem like we possess this place of authority in Christ, but if you are saved and are filled with His Spirit, I can assure you that the Lamb now sits upon the throne of your heart. We may not yet be perfected, but God calls those things that do not exist as though they did (see Rom. 4:17).

In the natural, we see lambs as weak little innocent creatures that need the help of another to protect them. For they could not and would not hurt anyone, for that is just their nature, and this is the picture that the Lord wants us to come away with when we see the Lamb upon the throne. "Fall on us and hide us from the presence of Him who sits on the throne, and from the wrath of the Lamb" (Rev. 6:16, NASU). Lambs have no wrath! That is the picture God wants us to see, for His wrath was appropriated in Christ as a Lamb slain from the foundation of the world. For God's wrath was finished on the cross two thousand years ago. Aren't we glad! Now He asks of us, "Will you take on the nature of the Lamb of God and take away the wrath of sin that is on the lives of those who do not know the nature of God, which is like a Lamb that takes away all the sin of the world?" Not just our sin, but every person who ever lived and will ever live throughout eternity. Praise His name forevermore!

It was King David who said, "Know that the Lord Himself is God; it is He who has made us, and not we ourselves; we are His people and the sheep of His pasture" (Ps. 100:3, NASU). God is the one who called us to be sheep and to be humble lambs like we are to be as little children in trusting Him in all things. The question that I have for myself is, Am I becoming humble like the lamb? Or am I like a stubborn old sheep that has not learned the ways of the Lamb of God? Just as marriage makes us one with our spouse, so are we to be with the Lamb of God having His likeness. This statement of the Lamb upon the throne is used several times in the book of Revelation.

> And they cry out with a loud voice, saying, "Salvation to our God who sits on the throne, and to the Lamb." (Rev. 7:10, NASU)

> For the Lamb in the center of the throne will be their shepherd, and will guide them to springs of the water of life; and God will wipe every tear from their eyes. (Rev. 7:17, NASU)

> To Him who sits on the throne, and to the Lamb, be blessing and honor and glory and dominion forever and ever. (Rev. 5:13, NASU)

His throne is in us because that is where He is to be seated. His throne is not some stationary place on some planet; it is a spiritual realm where God sees, knows, and hears all. Just as we the church are called the body of Jesus, being one with Him, so it should not be difficult for us to see ourselves taking on the nature of the Lamb so that we may all be like the Lamb upon the throne of creation to serve and love His creation.

Learning from the Lamb

Take My yoke upon you and learn from Me, for I am
gentle and humble in heart, and *you will find rest for your
souls*. (Matt. 11:29, NASU, emphasis mine)

How is it that the God of all creation would humble Himself
so low that He would identify Himself as a lamb? I personally
have no problem being called a lamb. I can use all the help I can
get in all areas of my life. But the almighty God Who is gentle
and humble of heart? Wow! He could have likened Himself to
a more forceful animal like a bull, elephant, dinosaur, or a goat,
but no, He identifies with a lowly creature. What a God we serve
that would invite us to learn His ways of humility, which is lowly
compared to the prideful ways of man. "These *[the overcomers]*
are the ones who follow the Lamb wherever He goes" (Rev. 14:4,
NASU, emphasis mine).

The only way for us to become like the Lamb is to follow the
Lamb throughout our lifetime upon the earth. Living through
His Spirit life here and now following the Lamb is the only
training ground that will make us into the image of Christ. This
is the way of the Lamb, which is never an easy road, but the
narrow, which is the way of sacrificing of our own will for His.

And I saw something like a sea of glass mixed with fire,
and those who had been victorious over the beast and his
image and the number of his name, standing on the sea

of glass, holding harps of God. And they sang the song of Moses, the bond-servant of God, and the song of the Lamb, saying,

> "Great and marvelous are Your works,
> O Lord God, the Almighty;
> Righteous and true are Your ways,
> King of the nations!
> "Who will not fear, O Lord, and glorify Your name?
> For You alone are holy;
> For ALL THE NATIONS WILL COME AND
> WORSHIP BEFORE YOU,
> FOR YOUR RIGHTEOUS ACTS HAVE BEEN
> REVEALED."
> (Rev. 15:2–4, NASU)

We who are called as overcomers in Christ sing the song of deliverance of Moses and the victory song of the Lamb through the midst of our trials and not just after them. Just as the children of Israel should have worshipped God at the Red Sea before it opened before them, for it was not until they crossed over that they then decided to break out with praise and thanksgiving. But we who have learned the ways of the Lamb have learned to worship Him in the midst of tribulation, having become victorious over our enemy, who is the revelation of evil, three in one.

1. The beast: the untamed evil nature in us that we fight against every day of our lives. Jesus was born in a barn among the beasts, so is He in our hearts.

2. His image: the likeness of the devil that the world portrays for us to be like rather than what we know Jesus is like.

3. The number of his name: having the number of his name 666 is for people to come into the full likeness of evil man rather than Christ. Man was made on the sixth day, which is the number of man. Three is the number of completeness as is the Father, Son, and Holy Spirit. It is now harvest time. We are either becoming like the seed of Christ, the three-in-one godhead, or we are coming into the likeness of the evil seed of the three in one. Today as I write this, there was the worst shooting in United States history just up a few miles from us in Orlando, Florida, that killed forty-nine people by a Muslim terrorist. Now that is the fullness of evil! These acts of evil are the triune works of the devil in the flesh. We make conscious decisions every day whether we are going to serve the nature of Christ or not.

At this time we must be people of peace that stand on the sea of glass and overcome all the evil that is trying to overcome us. We just don't have God on our side; we have Him on the inside! As we seek Him for direction in our lives, He is going to guide us into all truth, and in the truth we have peace and protection from the enemy. This is what it means to be standing on the sea of glass, peace in the midst of the storm. We are the victorious overcomers in Christ!

THE DELIVERERS ARE COMING!

For the earnest expectation of the creature waiteth for
the manifestation of the sons of God....*Because the
creature itself also shall be delivered from the bondage of
corruption* into the glorious liberty of the children of
God. For we know that *the whole creation groaneth and
travaileth in pain* together until now.

—Romans 8:19, 21–22 (KJV), emphasis mine

God's deliverers are coming! They are coming like a mighty army to set all men and creation free from the bondage of sin and death, for all creation is *groaning* to be freed from the curse of sin. No longer will man have to fear man. No longer will the animals have to sit and be watchful of their predators in fear of being harmed. Isaiah 65:25 will actually come to pass: "The wolf and the lamb shall graze together." One day there will be peace in the earth because there will be peace on the *inside* of man. *The Lamb of God within man and the beast nature within man will lay down together in peace*! But until this day comes to pass, there will be wars and rumors of wars in the earth because people are at war within themselves! The flesh wars against the Spirit continually. When there is peace within the heart of man, there will be peace in the earth. When Jesus comes to conquer every man, there will be peace in the earth. This is when He comes to set up His kingdom within the hearts of all people. We are truly living in an exciting time in the history of mankind!

I believe that America, in part, has been and is a forerunner to the coming deliverers of peace in the earth. What do I mean by this? Whenever America has gone to war, it has been for the purpose of setting other people free from oppressive governments. Think about it. The Revolutionary War was about freedom from Britain's tyranny, just as the Civil War was to set the black man free from slavery. World War I and II were about freeing people from oppression also. In fact, the American soldiers were called "the American liberators!"

In recent years, America has gone to war with Iraq to free the Kuwaiti people and to free Afghanistan from the Taliban religious leaders. I am not saying that America is always right in what they do or that it is always God's perfect will in what they are doing, only that they stand for the freedom of mankind! In the hearts of many people around the world, America stands for freedom. So also will the kingdom of God be to all peoples and nations one day, but much, much more! Not only will the kingdom of God set all people free from oppressive governments, but when the sons of God have been fully manifested, Jesus will set all people free from the bondage of all sin and death. *"Where the Spirit of the Lord is, there is liberty!"* The Spirit of the Lord will fully reign in all people one day, and when the Spirit of the Lord is fully manifested, there will be no sin, no sickness, or death at all! Hallelujah!

> *Let the saints rejoice in this honor* and sing for joy on their beds. May the praise of God be in their mouths and a double-edged sword [the Word] in their hands, to inflict vengeance on the nations and punishment on the peoples, to bind their kings [the man of sin] with fetters, their nobles with shackles of iron, to carry out the sentence written against them. *This is the glory [honor] of all His saints.* Praise the LORD. (Ps. 149:5–9, NIV, emphasis mine)

The sons of God are foreordained to rule and reign on the earth; this is God's eternal decree. "But the saints of the Highest One *will receive* the kingdom and *possess the kingdom forever, for all ages to come*" (Dan. 7:18, NASB, emphasis mine). But for this to happen, we must first be *called, chosen,* and *faithful.* Salvation is a free gift to everyone who will receive it. But for us to receive the inheritance of the kingdom, we first must be faithful servants. What king in the world would give the authority of his kingdom to anyone that did not prove his faithfulness first? Yes, our testings and trials are hard right now, but they are not in vain; there *is* a purpose to it all, and there *is* a Master Designer of our lives. His will and purpose is being done right *now* in our daily lives. Even as the earth and the universe have an order to them, so do our lives! The problem with us is that the plan of God is far too vast for our minds to comprehend. Like the universe, we can in no way understand it! God's ways are tried and true, and

His will can be trusted, as we see His faithfulness every day with the rising of the sun.

I am convinced that God allows this sinful world to go on because over the ages, He has not found enough faithful people in the earth to fulfill His purposes. But when He does find them, He will send Jesus back with them to establish His kingdom within the hearts of all men. "Do not harm the earth or the sea or the trees, *until we have sealed the bond-servants of our God on their foreheads.* And I heard the number of those who were sealed, one hundred and forty-four thousand sealed from every tribe of the sons of Israel" (Rev. 7:3–4, NASB, emphasis mine). God has a quota to fill, and the number He is looking for is 144,000 faithful ones. Whether this is a literal number or not, I do not know. All I know is, this world will go on until God finds His faithful sons, His precious fruit of the earth! It will be as it was in the days of Othniel: "And when the children of Israel cried unto the LORD, *the* LORD *raised up a deliverer to the children of Israel, who delivered them, even Othniel* [meaning 'mighty force of God'] the son of Kenaz, Caleb's younger brother. And the spirit of the LORD came upon him, and he judged Israel, and *went out to war:* and the LORD delivered Chushanrishathaim king of Mesopotamia into his hand; *and his hand prevailed against Chushanrishathaim* [meaning 'double wickedness']" (Judges 3:9–10, KJV, emphasis mine). The man of sin in us is the man of "double wickedness" that we all need deliverance from! The "mighty force of God" (His sons) will prevail over him, as did Othniel.

And *the armies which are in heaven*, clothed in fine linen, white and clean, *were following Him on white horses*. (Rev. 19:14, NASB, emphasis mine)

Our mighty Deliverer, Jesus, is about to be released from heaven, riding His white horse. Those who are like Him will help Him deliver mankind from this man of sin that has plagued mankind ever since the fall in the garden. No one physical man is the man of sin, but the *evil one* that lives within the heart of every human that has ever been born. This untamable beast in man will finally be slain by the Man of peace riding on the white horse into the heart of every man. Peace will then rule in the heart of every person. Hallelujah! Ephesians 2:14–16 (emphasis mine) will have come to pass:

> *For he himself is our peace*, who has made the two one [the man of sin and Jesus] and has destroyed the barrier [of sin], the dividing wall of hostility, by abolishing in his flesh the law with its commandments and regulations. *His purpose was to create in himself one new man out of the two, thus making peace*, and in this one body to reconcile both of them to God through the cross, by which he put to death their hostility.

Moses had a particular calling on him—the calling of a deliverer. His preparation was forty years in the wilderness after he had refused to be called a son of Pharaoh's daughter. We must learn from the experiences of Moses and his preparation to be a deliverer of the Lord's people. The calling of a deliverer is truly a noble one, but is the price one has to pay worth it? Moses did not even know what his full calling was when he was suffering those many years in the desert. He just thought he had failed in his deliverance ministry, and that was his lot in life. Moses had to come to the end of his self-life in order to trust God completely. God had a much higher calling on Moses than he could even conceive, and now, he is in glory forever to rule and reign with Christ. Moses was the meekest man that ever lived. Because of this, he was also the most powerful man to live other than Jesus. The word *meek* in the Hebrew means "to be humble, lowly, and crushed." *We can do nothing great for God until we have suffered greatly with Him in His sufferings.*

In this wonderful Old Testament recording of Moses, we have a prophetic picture of the sons of God working in league with their elder brother Jesus, just as Moses and Aaron were brothers working together to free Israel from bondage. Aaron was Moses's prophet, just as the church is Jesus's prophet or spokesman. Moses and Aaron were two witnesses in the land of Egypt. Egypt is a type of the world system that is holding many of God's people in bondage to the system of man. It is interesting to note that Aaron's name means "light bearer." That is what we are to be in this dark world, "light or truth bearers." Moses was a type of Jesus Christ, and Aaron was a type of the church. Did not Jesus say, "Truly, truly, I say to you, he who believes in Me, the works that I do shall he do also; and greater works than these shall he do; because I go to the Father" (John

14:12)? Yes, Jesus will do the greater works through His people because He has saved the best wine till last.

The Delivered Ones

God's perfect will for all of His creation is to give them full liberty and freedom from the curse of sin and death. But first, He must have a people completely free from the power of sin and death before they can set others free. Just because we are saved and sanctified by the blood of Jesus does not mean that we are living free from all bondage to sin. In fact, the opposite might be true! While most Christians seem to be in bondage to the same things that the world is, it is even worse because they are in bondage to the traditions of man's religions' doctrines, which hinders them from knowing the greater truths of God's word. How can we set other people free from the bondage of sin if we are in bondage to the same thing they are? We cannot! We must be totally set free from all that is binding us, then we will be able set others free! What Jesus said of the Pharisees is true of us today, if we are not walking in the truth. We will fall into the "pit" of religion, and once you're in it, it is hard to get out! "Let them alone; they are blind guides of the blind. And if a blind man guides a blind man, *both will fall into a pit*" (Matt. 15:14, KJV, emphasis mine).

Now the question is, how can we be set free from all sin and religion? By denying ourselves, picking up our cross daily, and following Jesus, that's how! We are to be walking victoriously through our trials and tribulations without losing heart or fainting. Jesus said in Revelation 3:18 that we are to buy truth from Him through our obedience to His will. We are to pay the price of picking up our cross daily and following Him! The Lord will lead us through many dark and trying days where we will have to completely trust Him and His word to bring us through, or we will lose our mind! We will not be able to see the next step in front of us, but this is how the Lord will lead us into His great victories and truths.

The man of sin in us will be overcome and slain; otherwise, the word of God would have never proclaimed that there are a people who will be victorious over the beast. "And I saw, as it were, a sea of glass mixed with fire, and *those who had come off victorious from the beast and from his image and from the number of his name,* standing on the sea of glass, holding harps of God" (Rev. 15:2, NASB, emphasis mine). There is a group of people in heaven and in earth who are victorious over the power of the flesh, the devil, and the world; and with the help of God's presence, we will be called the "overcomers"! John wrote of them in 1 John 2:13, "I am writing to you, fathers, because you know Him who has been from the beginning. I am writing to you, young men, *because you have overcome the evil one* [within and without]…the prayer of Jesus is being fulfilled. Deliver us from the evil one."

Yes, the evil one is the devil. But the evil one is also the seed of Satan that is *in us* that wars against us daily. This is the seed of Cain, who killed his brother, the righteous one. These two brothers are a natural type of what happened to Adam and Eve spiritually in the Garden of Eden. Satan, who is the aboriginal man of sin, slew the righteous man in Adam. Abel means "breath." The breath (presence) of God left Adam and Eve when they sinned and lost their fellowship with God. Cain's name means "to acquire or to take possession of." And this is what Cain did. He took away Abel's life (breath)!

The Cain *within us* must be slain if we are to be numbered with the overcomers! He is the original man of sin that wants to kill righteous Abel (Jesus) that lives in us. The Apostle John said that Cain was of the evil one, "not as Cain, *who was of the evil one*, and slew his brother. And for what reason did he slay him? Because *his deeds were evil*, and *his brother's were righteous* [Jesus]" (1 John 3:12, NASB, emphasis mine).

We must ask ourselves, why does God allow this world of sin and death to continue? He lets it go on in *hope*! "For the creation was subjected to futility, not of its own will, but because of Him who subjected it, *in hope*" (Rom. 8:20, NASB, emphasis mine). Hope for a people that will overcome the enemy within themselves by following His lead and example in the scriptures.

Dwelling in the Heavenlies

And [Jesus] *raised us up with Him* [in Spirit], and seated us with Him *in* the heavenly places, in Christ Jesus.

—Ephesians 2:6, emphasis mine

There are people in the earth that will arise into the heavenlies and will overcome this man of sin. The man of sin is the cause of all the world's sin and woes. He is earthy and demonic. He lives and reigns *in us* if we are living an earthbound life, only looking to the things of the earth rather than looking above where we are *already* seated with Christ! "If then you *have been raised up with Christ* [in the heavenlies], keep seeking the things above, where Christ is, seated at the right hand of God. *Set your mind on the things above*, not on the things that are on earth" (Col. 3:2, NASB, emphasis mine). We must arise in the spirit and walk in the heavenlies with Jesus if we are to set all men free. This will take much time and patience on our part to learn to walk in the ways of the Lord, but it will be worth it all in the end! It's much like road construction. At the time they are doing it, it is difficult, but when they are finished, it is well worth it!

For us to live in the heavenlies is similar to the way Jesus lived out of the physical realm and the heavenly realm at the same time. "And no man hath ascended up to heaven, but he that came down from heaven, even the Son of man which is *in* heaven" (John 3:13, KJV, emphasis mine). Jesus was "in" heaven while He was standing upon the earth! Jesus knew that He must only drink spiritually from His Father, the realm of life. The same can be true of us. When we are saved and filled with the Holy Spirit, we have a direct connection with God in the Spirit and can live out of both realms at the same time, receiving our strength and wisdom from God while we live in the natural.

Paul said in Ephesians 2:6 (emphasis mine), "And [Jesus] *raised us up with Him* [in Spirit], and seated us with Him *in* the heavenly places, in Christ Jesus." Most Christians are waiting to go to heaven when they die. But the truth is, we can have heaven *now* on earth! God's presence is what makes heaven, heaven. *"In His presence is fullness of joy!"* If God's presence were not in heaven, it would be like hell no matter how nice it was. For example, movie stars have the best of everything, yet many of their lives are a living hell because God's presence is not manifested in their lives. On the other hand, you could find a street person living in a cardboard shack with the presence of God, and it would be like heaven itself. Why? Because he has learned to live out of the realm of God! If we are going to make it through these days ahead, we too must learn to live out of the Spirit of God, finding our strength and joy from and in Him daily. "But I say, walk by the Spirit, and you will not carry out the desire of the flesh" (Gal. 5:16).

We must be very careful in our heavenly walk though, for like Lucifer, we too can fall from the heavenlies and forfeit our calling if we are walking after the ways of the flesh. "How art thou *fallen from heaven, O Lucifer, son of the morning*! How art thou cut down to the ground, which didst weaken the nations" (Isa. 14:12, KJV, emphasis mine)! The name Lucifer is Latin; it is not in the Hebrew scriptures. It means "brightness or the morning star." It is very closely related to Aaron's name, "light bearer." The name Lucifer is used only one time in the King James Version, and many Christians have interpreted him to be Satan before His fall from heaven. This could be true, but I believe that it was Adam who was the "light bearer" for God in the garden of Eden.

Before his fall, Adam was heavenly minded, but he became earthly minded and a mortal man after his treason against God. As Christians, we are called to have the morning star within us (Jesus)! We are to be "light bearers" or *Lucifers,* if you will, in a world of darkness. Jesus said in Revelation 2:28 that He will give us the morning star (Lucifer). I know that this will make many people very uncomfortable, but it is the truth!

We must learn to put on the knowledge of the Lord Jesus Christ and walk in His brightness/likeness. The word is our garment of light that will set us free and make us like Him. "Bless the LORD, O my soul! O LORD my God, Thou art very great; *Thou art clothed with splendor and majesty, covering Thyself with light as with a cloak,* stretching out heaven like a tent curtain" (Ps. 104:1–2, NASB, emphasis mine).

The enemy of our soul wants to cast us to the earth so that we become worldly minded rather than being heavenly minded. Revelation 12:4 says, "And his [Satan's] tail [lies] swept away a third of the stars [sons] of heaven, and threw them to the earth." Satan's "tail" is his "long tales," his lies and deceptions that he uses to deceive mankind. The true servants of God are the "stars" that Satan is trying to cast down to the earth so that they will become earthly minded. "The seven *stars* are the angels [messengers] of the seven churches" (Rev. 1:20). Even though we are called to be God's shining stars, many are falling from

COME TO THE GARDEN

being heavenly minded. Their love for the world is growing more and more with the passing of every day while their love for God is growing cold. "Because of the increase of wickedness, the love of most *will grow cold*" (Matt. 24:12, NIV, emphasis mine). We must be on guard for this attack from the enemy!

I had a dream that I was flying in a hot-air balloon fit for one person. I was flying nicely through the air, when all at once the air pressure was pushing me back down. I tried to go back up but got caught in the highline wires. I had to untangle myself while fighting the air pressure that was trying to ground me. Then I found myself in a large building in the hot-air balloon. The building was old and dirty, and I saw homeless people sleeping on the floor. When they woke up, they were angry with me because I was trying to help them. I then flew out the door in my balloon, and one of them cut it, but I was still able to fly away.

This is my interpretation: When we are to fly in the heavenlies with Jesus, demonic activity is all around us. The enemy is the god of the air (power in the air), and he puts pressures on us to keep us earthly minded and bound to this world. If we try to rise up in faith, he entangles us with *highline* distractions (things that seem important). "Therefore, since we are surrounded by such a great cloud of witnesses, *let us throw off everything that hinders and the sin that so easily entangles*, and let us run with perseverance the race marked out for us. *Let us fix our eyes on Jesus*, the author and perfecter of our faith, who for the joy set before him endured the cross, scorning its shame, and sat down at the right hand of the throne of God" (Heb. 12:1–2,

NIV, emphasis mine). The building was a place of depression and spiritual poverty, but when I escaped, the enemy came after me to destroy my faith so that I could not rise again. But I did! The Lord is showing us that we must keep the flames of the Holy Spirit burning in us so that we can keep our hot-air balloon flying high in the heavenlies with Jesus! If we are going to come up into the high places that God has for us in the spirit we have to set our goal (sights) on it (the fullness of God)! No one ever hit a goal without aiming for it! We must go higher into the things of God if we are going to become like Him!

MOVING THE MOUNTAIN OF TRUTH

> Beloved, while I was making every effort to write you
> about our common salvation, I felt the necessity to
> write to you appealing that you contend earnestly *for the*
> *faith* which was once for all delivered to the saints....
> But you, beloved, building yourselves up on your *most*
> *holy faith*; praying in the Holy Spirit.
>
> —Jude 1:3, 20 (NASB), emphasis mine

> And the word of God kept on spreading; and the
> number of the disciples continued to increase greatly
> in Jerusalem, and a great many of the priests were
> becoming obedient to *the faith*.
>
> —Acts 6:7 (NASB), emphasis mine

When the Bible speaks of "the faith" in these verses, it is not speaking about *faith* for God to answer our prayers, even though in some places of the Bible this is so. What Jude is writing about is the full aspect of the *Christian faith*; these are the truths that Jesus came to give us spiritual understanding in. "Who will have all men to be saved, *and to come unto the knowledge of the truth*" (1 Tim. 2:4, KJV, emphasis mine). "The knowledge of

the truth" is a very broad subject that we will spend our entire
lives seeking. Truth is a three-dimensional subject that we will
seek to understand its great depths throughout eternity. The
"truth" includes our salvation, which is the Passover experience;
speaking in other tongues, which is the Pentecost experience;
and the Feast of Tabernacles, which is us possessing the fullness
of God. We are to become knowledgeable and obedient to the
truth!

> Thus says the LORD, "I will return to Zion and will dwell
> in the midst of Jerusalem [God's sons]. Then Jerusalem
> will be called *the City of Truth, and the mountain of the*
> LORD of hosts will be called the Holy Mountain." (Zech.
> 8:3, NASB, emphasis mine)

The *truth* of the kingdom of God is like a great mountain
in the spirit realm that we are climbing throughout our lifetime
after we are saved. In fact, we do not start climbing *the mountain
of truth* until we have come to know Jesus as Lord and Savior.
He is the key to the knowledge of truth, and without Him, there
is no truth because He is the "Truth." Jesus said to the teachers
of the Law, "Woe to you lawyers! For you have taken away *the
key of knowledge* [Jesus]; you did not enter in yourselves, and
those who were entering in you hindered" (Luke 11:52, NASB,
emphasis mine). We must follow Jesus to the top of Mount
Zion and be changed into His likeness; at the top there will
be the wedding of the Lamb to His bride. "And I looked, and
behold, the Lamb was *standing on Mount Zion*, and with Him

one hundred and forty-four thousand, having His name and the name of His Father written on their foreheads [His name is His likeness and character]" (Rev. 14:1, NASB, emphasis mine). The ones having reached the top of the mountain had their minds renewed by the truth, which is the full likeness of their beloved Groomsman.

Below I have made a type of what I believe Mount Zion could look like in the spirit as we climb and learn its wonderful truths.

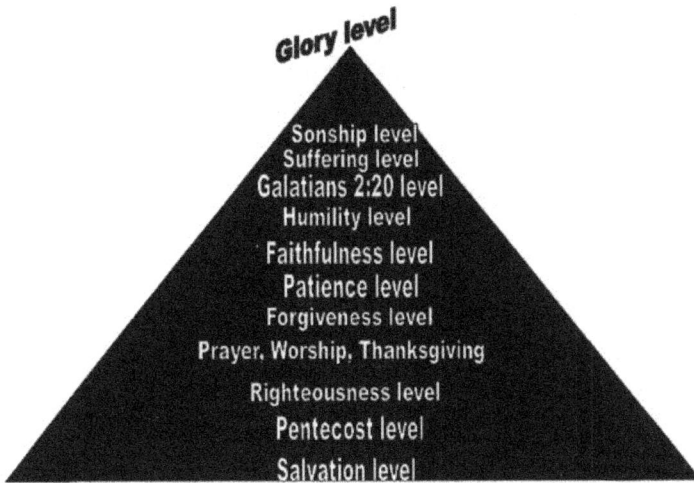

Glory level

Sonship level
Suffering level
Galatians 2:20 level
Humility level
Faithfulness level
Patience level
Forgiveness level
Prayer, Worship, Thanksgiving
Righteousness level
Pentecost level
Salvation level

Learning present truth can prove to be very difficult for our religious and traditional mind-set because the ways of the past are so ingrained in us. We like to hold on to what we were first taught, what we feel comfortable with, and because Pastor, Dr., or Reverend So and So taught us these things, believing it himself. The higher we climb the mountain of truth, the greater others in the religious system will fight against the truth that is in us because they cannot understand it. They will try to reason with us, attempting to stop us on our journey upward into the high places of God, even as they did Christian in the *Pilgrim's Progress* book. They want us to follow them back into their religious prison camps to die with them there. But we were never told to follow a person to the top of the Mount Zion, only the Lamb! We are not to be *taken captive or held prisoner* by anyone's denominational traditions that hold us to one level of *the mountain of truth*. We must move higher and higher upward to the fullness of God. "*See to it that no one takes you captive* [prisoner] through hollow [shallow] and *deceptive philosophy* [doctrines], *which depends on human tradition* and the basic principles of this world rather than on Christ" (Col. 2:8, NIV, emphasis mine).

As a small boy, I was raised in the Lutheran church and grade school. Lutheranism was all that I knew about God and the truths of the Bible. As far as I knew, everyone in the world believed as a Lutheran! Then one day I heard about "those Baptists," who did not let their children go to dances. When I heard this, I thought, *Thank God I'm Lutheran, they don't care if I go to the dance or not!* It did not matter what God thought about dancing as long the Lutherans okayed it. Then it was all right with me. My mind had been controlled by Lutheran doctrines that I once learned as a little boy, not the Word and Spirit of God. But that was about to be challenged by the Spirit of truth when I received Him into my heart.

To learn present truth can be very fearful to us as we climb this mountain of God because we are afraid of change and of the unknown. We want to feel secure in what we are doing and what we believe to be the truth of God. When our present understanding is challenged, we react with contempt and put up walls of protection around us so that nothing can bring harm to our belief system. Feelings of fear and insecurity will always grip us when we are presented with truth that we have not heard before.

We felt fear when we first came to Jesus because it was unknown to us; again we were fearful when we received the baptism in the Holy Spirit. This is how it will be when we are presented with any truths that we have not heard before. Our present insecurities originate from the fall of man in the garden. As we began to eat of the tree of the knowledge of good and evil, it made the truth of God seem foolish and fearful to our carnal mind. Adam and Eve became fearful of God and hid themselves from the truth that He is. The fear that we all feel can only be changed through our receiving and understanding truth. "And the one on whom seed [the truth] was sown on the good soil [a person], this is the man who *hears the word and understands it*" (Matt. 13:23, NASB, emphasis mine). The higher we climb the mountain of truth and understanding in spiritual things, the more we can overcome our enemy's schemes of using deception to defeat us because we will understand spiritual realities better and foil his plans against us. Our knowledge and understanding of truth *must be stretched* in us for us to be growing and going up the mountain. Growing in truth will make us feel uncomfortable at times. When we grew in our physical bodies, we had pains, and so it is in our spiritual life also. As young children, we could not wait to grow up; so now, we also must desire to grow up spiritually! This is not a calling for the halfhearted Christian, but for those who have a passionate love for Jesus and desire to be one with Him at the top of the mountain, ones who are willing to pay any price to be with Him! Once our minds are totally renewed with the truth, we will be transformed into the likeness and character of Jesus. But this will only come about slowly, line upon line, truth upon truth, even as one would climb a mountain through perseverance.

When we asked Jesus to baptize us with the Spirit of truth, we received the down payment or deposit of what is yet to come in our heart. "Set his seal of ownership on us, *and put his Spirit in our hearts as a deposit, guaranteeing what is to come*" (2 Cor. 1:22, NIV, emphasis mine). By no means was it the only payment we are to be given while still alive upon the earth. There are to be *many* deposits of the Holy Spirit placed into our heart; yes, even *daily* fillings of the Spirit of God. The New Revised Bible says that the initial filling was the "first installment." When we buy something on an installment plan, the first payment is just the beginning; there are more to follow! Hallelujah!

Some Christians seem to think that they have it all right away, but they do not. We must be prepared by the smaller impartations of the Spirit to be readied for the fullness of the Spirit. Please hear me, my friend. He *is* coming with a great outpouring. But only those who have prepared themselves for it and who are looking for Him will be ready! If we have not prepared ourselves by staying full of the Spirit, we will not be able to handle the fullness of the Spirit. We will be like an old wineskin that will explode with the new wine of the Spirit. Jesus desires to reveal Himself to us today in greater revelations of Himself in truth and by filling us with His Spirit as we spend time with Him and cry out to know Him more in truth.

God will give us greater installments of His Spirit and truth because we are asking to know Him more, but now we must not just ask to know Him more, but to know Him and possess Him unto *all* His fullness! Only receiving more of Him will make our lives worth living. Worldly people are pushing themselves to go farther and farther than anyone has ever gone before, like in sports, science, and technology. Now it's our turn to break through the realm of the flesh and push higher and higher into the high places of God's truth so that we are changed into the likeness of His life. To attain to these high places of truth will not be easy and will take great sorrow and suffering on our part, even as a natural mountain climber has to go through the many trials of his climb. But because of the glory of reaching the top, the climber does not quit because he has a chance to reach the summit that few people have ever done. It is a rarity to reach the top! What makes something valuable in the world like a diamond is its scarcity, and this is why the truth of God's word is such a treasure because so few of people have it! Paul called it "the unfathomable riches of Christ" (Eph. 3:8, NASB).

God is our very best friend, and He *will* lead us into all truth, but our insecurities will hinder us from growing in truth. As we learn more of God's truth and believe it, it will set us free from all our insecurities and give us greater peace through knowing His love. But when we say no to His revealed truth, we then will stay on the present level of truth that we are on. The wisest thing we can do when we are presented with new teachings that we do not understand is to sit on it. We should ask the Holy Spirit to teach us the truth in His time and not criticize it. We must continually ask the Holy Spirit to reveal in us any false doctrines of man and have it cleansed out of us by knowing truth.

I have found that He will work with me and reveal all truth to me as we were promised in John 16:13 (emphasis mine): "But when He, the Spirit of truth, comes, *He will guide you into all the truth*; for He will not speak on His own initiative, but whatever He hears, He will speak; and He will disclose to you what is to come." Our Christian faith is about knowing and growing in truth (Jesus) so that the truth will set us free from all lies and deceptions! Our growth in truth does not stop with our basic salvation experience, but it is to grow daily like a tree firmly planted by the river. A tree is either growing or dying; it cannot do both at the same time. So it is with our Christian faith.

The book *Hinds' Feet on High Places* by Hannah Hurnard speaks very clearly about what the mountainous high places are. I quote:

> Sometimes, as she looked on the glorious panorama visible from these lowest slopes (truths) in the Kingdom of Love, she found herself blushing as she remembered some of the dogmatic statements which she and others had made in the depths of the valley about the High Places and the ranges of Truth (deeper truths). They had been able to see so little and were so unconscious of what lay beyond and above. If that had been the case down in the valley, how much more clearly, she now realized, that even up on those wonderful slopes (deeper truths) *she was only looking out on a tiny corner of the whole.*
>
> She began to understand quite clearly *that truth cannot be understood from books alone* or by any written words, but *only by personal growth and development in understanding,* and that things written even in the Book of Books can be astonishingly misunderstood while one still lives on lower levels of spiritual experience (truths) and on the wrong side of the grave on the mountains.
>
> She perceived that no one who finds herself up on the slopes of the Kingdom of Love can possibly dogmatize (be opinionated) about what is seen there, because it is only then that she comprehend how small a part of the glorious whole she sees. All she can do is to grasp with wonder, awe, and thanks giving, and to long with all her heart *to go higher and to see and understand more.*
>
> Lord, that I might receive my sight! Help me to open myself to more light. Help me to fuller understanding.

Those who understand deeper spiritual truths are not any better than those who do not. The difference is that they have had more grace to mature in spiritual experiences and understanding. Someone that studies to be a lawyer is not any better than anyone else; it's just that they have disciplined and applied themselves to learn about law. An eighteen-year-old person that just graduated from high school is not any better than a ten-year-old child that hasn't; it's just that eighteen-year-old is more knowledgeable due to the years of study. We must not compare our spiritual maturity to anyone else least we fall into despair or pride for those who think they stand will fall! If we must compare ourselves to anyone, let's compare ourselves to Jesus! "For we dare not make ourselves of the number, or compare ourselves with some that commend themselves: but they measuring themselves by themselves, and comparing themselves among themselves, *are not wise*" (2 Cor. 10:12, KJV, emphasis mine).

Moving the Mountain

We must understand that this mountain of truth is the kingdom of God and that the kingdom dwells *within* us! As soon as we yield to the kingdom of God within our heart, our mind will be renewed by the truth that is within us because the King lives within each of us to teach and change us. Even when we have made it to the top and understand all spiritual truths, we are not called to stay and live there. *We are called to bring the truths of God back down the mountain to the people who are living in the valley below.* We must move this mountain of truth/faith that is within us by bringing it to all nations. Then they too can receive its rich bountiful blessings and be set free from sin and death by knowing the truth, for knowing the truth will set all free! "That the creation itself will be set free from its bondage to decay and will obtain the freedom of the glory [truth] of the children of God" (Rom. 8:21, NRSV).

> *But in the last days it shall come to pass*, that the mountain of the house of the LORD *shall be established in the top of the mountains* [governments], and it shall be exalted above the hills; and people shall flow unto it. And many nations shall come, and say, *Come, and let us go up to the mountain of the* LORD, and to the house of the God of Jacob; and *he will teach us of his ways, and we will walk in his paths*: for the law shall go forth of Zion [the church], and the word of the LORD from Jerusalem [God's sons]. (Mic. 4:1–2, KJV, emphasis mine)

Hallelujah, what a word! The nations are going to know His great truths and choose to walk His path of dying to self, just as the rest of His people had to do. The nations will be changed; we have His word on it!

> And Jesus answered and said to them, "Truly I say to you, if you have faith, and do not doubt, you shall not only do what was done to the fig tree, but even if you say to *this mountain, 'Be taken up and cast into the sea,'* it shall happen." (Matt. 21:21, NASB, emphasis mine)

To move a mountain sounds like great faith, and it is! Our Christian faith is *"this mountain"* that must be moved into the sea (nations)! The sea represents the peoples of the world that need the truths of God in order to be changed. "And he said to me, *'The waters* which you saw where the harlot sits, *are peoples and multitudes and nations and tongues"* (Rev. 17:15, NASB, emphasis mine). Spiritual Mount Zion is "this mountain" of truth that must be moved from the spirit realm to the earth where mankind lives so that they also may be changed by the Truth (Jesus) and partake of heavens bountiful treasures. "Thy kingdom come. Thy will be done, *On earth as it is in heaven* [or spirit]" (Matt. 6:10, NASB, emphasis mine). God will have His will done on earth as it is done in heaven because He has already spoken it forth!

> *On this mountain* [of truth] the LORD Almighty will prepare a feast of rich food [truth] *for all peoples*, a banquet of aged wine—the best of meats [the word] and the finest of wines [His Spirit]. *On this mountain* [of truth] *he will destroy the shroud that enfolds all peoples [the darkness blinding them], the sheet that covers all nations.* (Isa. 25:6–7, NIV, emphasis mine)

> For as ye have drunk *upon my holy mountain, so shall all the heathen drink continually*, yea, they shall drink, and they shall swallow down, and *they shall be as though they had not been*. But *upon mount Zion shall be deliverance*, and there shall be holiness; and the house of Jacob shall possess their possessions" (Obad. 1:16–17, KJV, emphasis mine)

There is soon coming a day when God will rip this veil of darkness covering all nations that prevents them from seeing the light of the glory of God. Then they will mourn because they will see that they had been living in His glory all the time without knowing it because they did not seek Him. "Look, he is coming with the clouds [His saints], and *every eye will see him* [spiritual eye], even those who pierced him; and *all* the peoples of the earth will mourn because of him. So shall it be! Amen" (Rev. 1:7, NIV, emphasis mine).

Come, Lord Jesus!

THE MYSTERY OF INIQUITY

For *the mystery* of iniquity doth already work.

—2 Thessalonians 2:7 (KJV), emphasis mine

The heart is more deceitful *than all else* and is desperately
sick; *who can understand it?*

—Jeremiah 17:9 (NASB)

Yes, who can understand the mystery of iniquity in the heart?
We can! God has given us the understanding in His word. Our
job is to find the truth as if we were looking for lost treasure.
Most people like a good mystery novel or movie to keep them
on the edge of their seat in suspense. But when it comes to *the
mystery of iniquity* (sin), they do not have a clue to its mystery or
where they may find the answers as to why sin is still reigning
in them after salvation. A mystery is something that is secretive
or hidden from the understanding of most people. Paul wrote
much about the mysteries of the kingdom of God so that we
might have understanding in spiritual truth.

Having made known unto us *the mystery* of his will, according to his good pleasure which he hath purposed in himself. (Eph. 1:9, KJV, emphasis mine)

How that by revelation he made known unto me *the mystery*; (as I wrote afore in few words, whereby, when ye read, ye may understand my knowledge in *the mystery of Christ*). (Eph. 3:3–4, KJV, emphasis mine)

The gospel message itself was even a mystery to the disciples of Jesus while He was ministering on the earth. When Jesus told them that He came to die on the cross, they were puzzled and even tried to hinder Him from going to Jerusalem to do so. We must understand that while Jesus did come to die on the cross for us, He also came to give us understanding in spiritual things wherein we are now living, things which we do not fully understand. "And He answered and said to them, 'To you it has been granted *to know the mysteries* of the kingdom of heaven, *but to them it has not been granted*" (Matt. 13:11, NASB, emphasis mine). Jesus came to give His called ones spiritual understanding in spiritual things, but to the rest of the world, it has not yet given. It was a mystery then and remains one now to most of the people alive!

If we are going to understand and overcome the mysterious power of sin that lives within us, we must first know that it is called by many different names in scripture, such as the flesh, the man of sin, the carnal nature, the spirit of disobedience, and the spirit of Antichrist. This spirit of sin has been reigning within every human being ever since the fall of man. "As for you, *you were dead* in your transgressions and sins, in which you used to live when you followed the ways of this world and of the ruler of the kingdom of the air, *the spirit who is now at work in those who are disobedient*" (Eph. 2:1–2, NIV, emphasis mine). Unless we understand that the spirit of sin is alive and well in our sin nature and that its desire is to fully control us, we will not overcome it because we will be blinded to the truth! God told Cain, "And if you do not do well, *sin is crouching at the door; and its desire is for you, but you must master it*" (Gen. 4:7, NASB, emphasis mine).

Many Christians falsely believe that when Jesus comes into their heart, the man of sin in them immediately dies, and they will never have to war against the flesh again. This kind of thinking will only prove fatal to their Christian growth. *The only way for sin to die in a Christian is for us to die to it daily.* This is why it is called "being crucified"—it hurts! Crucifixion is a very slow and painful way of dying. This is why so many of our sins just do not go away overnight; they must be starved out! Whatever we feed in us will grow! If it is sin, it will grow to overcome us. If we feed the seed of God that has been planted within us, *it* will grow to overcome the power of sin in us. We make daily choices upon what we feed.

I planted some grass seed in my front yard and watered it for weeks before the grass began to sprout and grow lushly. But soon after watering, I noticed that I had another problem—weeds! The same water that caused the good seed to grow also caused the weed seed to grow. The weed seed was already in the ground when I planted the good seed, but I could not see it. So instead of tearing up the lawn to plant the good seed over again, I decided to pull up the weeds one by one when they had grown. The Lord used this to speak to me about the garden of my heart. For years I had wondered how sin could still be in my life after twenty years of being saved and of planting the word of God daily in my heart. He began to show me that when we are first saved and filled with the Spirit, the emotional excitement in our spirit could carry us for several years. But after a while, our old nature and the sins of the past grow and creep back into our lives slowly. Jesus clearly warns us of this in Mark 4:18–19 (emphasis mine): "Still others, like seed sown among thorns, hear the word; but the worries of this life, the deceitfulness of wealth and the desires for *other things come in and choke the word, making it unfruitful.*" Don't you see? The seed of sin was always in our old nature (earth), even as the weed seed is in the ground, though we cannot see it until it is well watered and both the weed seed and the good seed grow together. "When the wheat sprouted and formed heads, *then the weeds also appeared*" (Matt. 13:26, NIV, emphasis mine). When God's seed is maturing in us and we are becoming more and more like Him, the weed seed at that time also begins to mature and appear in us, and we feel sinful because of it. This must not discourage us; God will have all the weeds pulled out of us!

I know that Jesus lives in me, I know that Jesus is growing in me, I also know that His Spirit is working mightily in me, but what I see in my outward flesh doesn't correspond with what I know is on the inside of me. We are seeing the chaff that lies on the surface, but we are failing to discern the fully ripe kernel of wheat that lies within! The chaff is removed on the threshing floor at the time of the harvest. The tares are torn out of the field and burned in the day of harvest. Don't mistake the kernel of wheat with the chaff or the tares with the wheat! Just because we have this treasure in earthen vessels doesn't mean that the value of the treasure within is diminished!

So what should we do? We must pull out the weeds one by one when they have grown! It's not until the weed has grown large enough that we can pull it out anyway. I believe the Lord allows us to fight with certain sins for a time in our life so we are sick and tired of seeing those ugly weeds and will turn to Him for help in pulling them out and crucifying them. Unless we hate our sin, we won't want it pulled out of the garden of our heart and instead could consider it to be a beautiful plant. In fact, I have heard of people planting weed seed in their yard because they thought it was pretty until the weeds took over their whole yard! We must keep our garden clean for the Lord for He is the only one that sees our garden, which is the place where we have daily fellowship with Him in spirit. We will certainly want to keep it clean for Him so that when He comes to walk in our garden, as he did with Adam, He will be pleased!

As Christians, we must understand how sin gets power over us. Jesus came to die on the cross to set us free from sin's power! "For sin shall not have dominion over you" (Rom. 6:14, KJV). It is written, "Sin will not have power over us!" But the truth of the matter is, *we* still allow sin to reign in us at times. Why is this?

James said, "Each one is tempted when, *by his own evil desire* [in his own heart], he is dragged away [controlled] and enticed [drawn into sin]. Then, after desire has conceived [been planted], it gives birth [grows] to sin; and sin, when it is *full-grown*, gives birth to death" (James 1:14–15, NIV, emphasis mine). Very simply, if we start a sin and let it grow like a weed, it will form into a habit, and that habit will grow into a controlling monster that we cannot control in our own power. Once this takes place, we will not be able to hide it any longer from others because the sin will have manifested from what was in our heart the whole time. As Christians, our desire should be to become like Jesus, going from glory level to glory level into His likeness. But our sin will cause us to come away *from* His glory rather than going up in levels, and our light of life will go out, causing us spiritual death. James goes on to say in verse 16, "Don't be deceived, my dear brothers." In other words, "Know and understand how sin can grow and progress in our life and destroy us!"

The progression of sin is fourfold:

1. We play with sin as if it is a cute rattlesnake, thinking it cannot harm us.
2. We reap a habit and advance in sin. It grows enough to require daily feeding.
3. We are then overcome by sin because it has grown into a large rattlesnake that bites us!
4. Then death comes to our spiritual life, and tragically, we have no fellowship with God.

When we get saved, there are two powerful forces living inside of us that want to rule our thought and emotional life. Either the spirit of sin or the Holy Spirit will control us. The daily choice is up to us as we obey the truth that is in Jesus Christ. "Jesus therefore was saying to those Jews who had believed Him, '*If you abide in My word*, then you are truly disciples of Mine; *and you shall know the truth, and the truth shall make you free*'" (John 8:31–32, NASB, emphasis mine). As we abide in the truth, the truth has the power to set and keep us free from the power of sin and bondage. It is written! But we must know how to wield the sword and apply the truth to our lives, fighting back after we are saved. The sword of the spirit (the word of God) will set us free from the soulish carnal realm. "For the word of God is living and active and sharper than any two-edged sword, and *piercing as far as the division of soul [flesh] and spirit*" (Heb. 4:12, NASB, emphasis mine). We must know and understand that the truth will set us free!

Knowing the Truth

We must first know that sin is addictive. It does not matter if you can drink it, snort it, smoke it, shoot it, or look at it. *All* sin is addictive because it lies dormant in the flesh (earth). Given the right circumstances, it can come to life and flourish whether we can get the drug or alcohol into our body or not! Drugs and alcohol is not the problem; quickened sin is! Lying, stealing, anger, gambling, evil words and thoughts, pornography, and all kinds of sexual sin is addictive because once it is started in our life, it must be fed to keep growing. As we continually feed it on a regular basis, it becomes a monster habit that we cannot handle or stop in our own power. We must know how to handle or exercise the word against the spirit of sin so that it does not get a hook in us. We must fight off these demonic powers that are manipulating our flesh over and over, just as Jesus did in the wilderness when He spoke back to the devil, "It is written!" We must also get away from whatever is causing us to sin; we must *flee* from temptation to be freed from its clutches. Temptation is nothing but an evil spirit that is trying to lure us into being addicted to sin.

The only way for us to combat sin in the flesh is for us to plant the word of God in our heart. When we obey it, it has the power to deliver us from powerful addictions in our soulish nature. "Therefore, *get rid of all moral filth* and the evil that is so prevalent and *humbly [be teachable and] accept the word planted in you, which can save [deliver] you.* Do not merely listen to the word, and so deceive yourselves. *Do what it says*" (James 1:21–22, NIV, emphasis mine). As we *do what the word says*, we will break free from the powerful addictions and habits of the soul, going through withdrawal symptoms because of our dependence on the sin. Remember, all sin is addictive, even false doctrines, because the sin nature wants to anchor itself into something other than God, even if it is a lie. When the power of sin is broken in our life through obedience to the word, our whole life will be shaken because our crutch in life is now broken. We were created to be addicted to God's presence alone, feeding upon His *every* word so that we are standing upon His sure foundation (the word), which cannot be shaken! As we speak the word out loud and obey it, the enemy and our soulish addictions must be broken because of the power of God's word. If God's word has the power to create life, what are our little addictions compared to that? We must quote scriptures to our adversary such as these:

> *"No weapon that is formed against you shall prosper,* and every tongue that accuses you in judgment you will condemn. This is the heritage of the servants of the LORD, and their vindication is from Me," declares the LORD. (Isa. 54:17, NASB, emphasis mine)

> What shall we then say to these things? *If God be for us, who can be against us?* (Rom. 8:31 KJV, emphasis mine)

> Nay, *in all these things we are more than conquerors* through him that loved us. (Rom. 8:37, KJV, emphasis mine)

> I can do all things through Christ which strengtheneth me. (Phil. 4:13, KJV)

> Ye are of God, little children, and have overcome them: because *greater is he that is in you, than he that is in the world.* (1 John 4:4, KJV, emphasis mine)

Now the question is, How do we deny our sinful desires in the heat of battle? Answer: by continuing to resist it! It may take a year or more to defeat it, but we will win in the long run *if* we do not give up! Sin never has to overcome a believer! Yet I must state, the longer we wait to defeat sin in our life, the longer it will take before our minds are renewed, and we move on into the maturity of Christ. In fact, if we do not fight the good fight of faith against sin, we could fight one certain sin for the rest of our life without maturing into His likeness. But if we will believe what the word already says, we can be free! "In him *you were also circumcised*, in the putting off of the sinful nature, not with a circumcision done by the hands of men but with the circumcision done by Christ" (Col. 2:11, NIV, emphasis mine). When we come to Jesus and repent of our sins, the Bible promises us that our old sinful nature *was* circumcised! The flesh has already been cut off; it is a done deal between God and you! Hallelujah! Now we must tell that to our head and live it out on a daily basis. We must stop warring against God inside of us, for this is Who we really are battling against anyway—light against darkness!

> Submit therefore to God. *Resist* the devil and *he will flee from you.* (James 4:7, NASB, emphasis mine)

> But *resist* him, firm in your faith, knowing that the same experiences of suffering are being accomplished by your brethren who are in the world. (1 Pet. 5:9, NASB, emphasis mine)

The word *resist* means "to stand or endure against." Resistance works for our good. The things that hinder us most only work to make us stronger even as a weight lifter pushes against his heavy weights. So God allows the devil to work against us to make us stronger spiritually. When we resist temptation, it only works to make us stronger as if we were a weight lifter in our spirit. As we resist temptation, we become stronger and stronger against it. But as we yield to our sin, we only become weaker and weaker, yielding to it the next time that we are tempted and finally being overcome by it.

"Jacob I Loved, but Esau I Hated" (Romans 9:13)

It has always been hard for me to understand in this verse why God hated Esau so much until I saw in scripture that Esau is a spiritual type of the flesh, the carnal man that is living in all of us. The story of Jacob and Esau is an allegory of the warring between the sin and spiritual natures within mankind, which will one day be defeated, just as it was when God wrestled with Jacob, and He changed him. Paul said that Isaac and Ishmael were also an allegory, "for it is written that Abraham had two sons [Isaac and Ishmael], one by the bondwoman and one by the free woman [Law and promise]....This is *allegorically* speaking: for these women are two covenants [Law and faith], one proceeding from Mount Sinai bearing children who are to be slaves [to sin]; she is Hagar....But what does the Scripture say? '*cast out the bondwoman and her son* [Law and sin], *for the son of the bondwoman [sin] shall not be an heir with the son of the free woman* [sons of God]" (Gal. 4:22, 24, 30; NASB; emphasis mine).

Isaac (the promise) and Ishmael (the law) fought against one another until they were separated by the word of the Lord. However, Jacob and Esau fought in the womb as to who would be first born. Our flesh (the sin nature) is the first born as Esau was, and God hated Esau! Our flesh and spirit (Jacob and Esau) have been warring inside of us against each other as these two did in the natural. Esau lived his whole life as a worldly man, and even though Jacob started out as a deceiver, God changed him and his name from *Jacob*, meaning "deceiver," to *Israel*, meaning "*he will rule as God* or as a prince of God" (a prince is a son in a royal family).

So it is with us, we are also promised a new name in Revelation 2:17: "I will give him a white stone, and a new name." As overcomers in this life, we are promised to rule and reign as the sons of God with Christ!

> But as many as received him, to them gave he power *to become the sons of God*, even to them that believe on his name. (John 1:12, KJV, emphasis mine)

> And hast *made us* unto our God kings and priests: and *we shall reign on the earth.* (Rev. 5:10, KJV, emphasis mine)

Before Ishmael was born, God named him and told Hagar that the boy would end up being a wild man against others. "And he will be a wild man; his hand will be against every man, and every man's hand against him; and he shall dwell in the presence of all his brethren" (Gen. 16:12, KJV). After Isaac was born, Ishmael gave in to his wild beast nature and started to persecute Isaac so much that Sarah became angry, insisting that Hagar and her son leave their household. "Wherefore she [Sarah] said unto Abraham, *Cast out* this bondwoman and her son: *for the son of this bondwoman shall not be heir with my son, even with Isaac....* And God said unto Abraham, Let it not be grievous in thy sight because of the lad, and because of thy bondwoman; in all that Sarah hath said unto thee, *hearken unto her voice; for in Isaac shall thy seed be called*" (Gen. 21:10, 12; KJV; emphasis mine).

God told Abraham to listen to what his wife said and cast out the bondwoman and her son because Ishmael *could not* receive the blessing of the inheritance along with the Isaac. What does this mean for us? Our old sinful nature, "the wild beast" (Ishmael), has been mocking and persecuting our spiritual life (faith), and the flesh cannot inherit the kingdom of God (the promise of sonship). "Now I say this, brethren, that *flesh and blood cannot inherit the kingdom of God*; nor does the perishable inherit the imperishable" (1 Cor. 15:50, NASB, emphasis mine). Neither Ishmael nor Esau could receive the inheritance from their father because they represented the old Adamic nature, the flesh! And neither will we, if we are like them and living for the things of the flesh or the world. "For you know that even afterwards, when he [Esau] desired to inherit the blessing, *he was rejected*, for he found no place for repentance, though he sought for it with tears" (Heb. 12:17, NASB, emphasis mine).

Notice that God told Abraham to "cast out" the woman and her son. God did not do it for him; rather, He gave Abraham the authority of His word to cast them out of his household. We also must "cast out" of our household (our body) the bondwoman (the old Law) and her son (sin) if we want to inherit the promise! God has given us the authority in His word to cast out of ourselves the Law and sin and to *cleanse* ourselves with the power of His word. "If a man *cleanses* [casts out of] himself from the latter [fleshly and worldly things], he will be an instrument for noble purposes, made holy, useful to the Master and prepared to do any good work [the work of sonship]" (2 Tim. 2:21, NIV, emphasis mine) (see also Col. 3:9–10 and Rom. 13:12–14). We must cleanse or "cast out" of ourselves the man of sin through the power of God's word. God will not do it for us. He said, "*Cast out* the bondwoman and her son!" (Law and the seed of sin). We must "cast out" the seed of the serpent that has been crawling around in us ever since the fall of man. For it is written, "The great dragon *was cast out*, that old serpent, called the Devil, and Satan, which deceiveth the whole world: he was *cast out* into the earth, and his angels were *cast out* with him" (Rev. 12:9, KJV, emphasis mine).

We have been given a marvelous command by God to "cast out" sin and can do it through the help of Michael's and God's word (see Rev. 12:7). The name *Michael* means "who is like God." In other words, those "who are like God in character" will be given the grace to overcome and "cast out" the enemy and defeat sin in the flesh (mind). We are told in 2 Corinthians

10:4–5 (emphasis mine), "For the weapons [the word] of our warfare are not carnal, *but mighty through God* to the pulling down of strong holds [in the mind]; *Casting down imaginations,* [arguments in the mind] and every high thing that exalteth itself against the knowledge of God [the truth], and *bringing into captivity every thought* to the obedience of Christ." Indeed our mind will be renewed by the power of God's word and Spirit, and we will reign with Christ for one thousand years on earth. If we desire the full revelation of Jesus Christ in us, casting out our sin is a *must,* for that alone will bring forth the fulfillment to the promise of God! This is the perfect will of God for us!

> And I heard a loud voice saying in heaven, *Now is come salvation* [full deliverance from sin has come], and strength, and the kingdom of our God, and the power of his Christ: for *the accuser of our brethren is cast down,* which accused them before our God day and night. And *they overcame him [cast him out] by the blood of the Lamb, and by the word of their testimony; and they loved not their lives unto the death.* (Rev. 12:10–11, KJV, emphasis mine)

When the man of sin is "cast out" of us, the "accuser" that lives within us will also be cast out! The "accuser" is another name for the seed of the serpent that lives within us because he accuses us day and night before God. To *accuse* means "to charge with a shortcoming or wrongdoing." God lives within our heart, and our enemy (the flesh) that lives within us is always trying to bring a voice of condemnation on us to make us feel guilty or bad about our performance as a Christian. We must not let his voice of lies within us deceive us any longer. We *must* resist his lies through the power of our testimony (God's word). The word *brethren* means "one that is connected or is a kinsmen." Other than the Lord, the man of sin living in us is our closest kin; these two are continually warring against one another until the man of sin is completely cast out!

Satan is the master deceiver of the ages, and if possible, he will always try to deceive us in different ways. One of his most effective and deadly deceptions is not outward sin, but inward accusations! There is a reason why he is called "the accuser of the brethren...who accuses them before our God day and night." The man of sin works within us ceaselessly to try and hinder us from coming into the likeness of Jesus. The accuser within us says, "You're not good enough for God, you have sinned too much, God can't forgive you. Give up, you're a failure at the Christian life. You don't pray enough, you're no good, nobody likes you, you're ugly, God cannot love you." His accusations *within* us go on daily as he tries to defeat us *within* our own heart! These vain imaginations within us *must* stop! We must condemn and overcome the voice of our accuser within ourselves and cast him out! "Every tongue that accuses you in judgment *you will condemn.*" If God is revealing the accuser to us at this time, it is so that we will recognize him and overcome him. There will be a people in these end times that will cast him down and out of themselves; these are the overcomers! To overcome our accuser, we must use these three methods to defeat him: (1) salvation

COME TO THE GARDEN

(deliverance) through the blood of Jesus, (2) our testimony (the word of God), and (3) dying daily to the self-life.

> For to be carnally minded is death; but to be spiritually minded is life and peace. *Because the carnal mind is enmity against God*: for it is not subject to the law of God, neither indeed can be. (Rom. 8:6–7, KJV, emphasis mine)

The word *enmity* here means "to be as an enemy and adversary like Satan!" When we are living by our own fleshly reasoning, we are agreeing with our "accuser" and are living out of our carnal nature rather than living in the truth of God's word. We are to live by every word that proceeds out of the mouth of God.

I believe that at this time in history, God is giving His elect great grace to "cast out" the seed of the serpent, and *if* we will obey Him, we too will become *"the Israel of God,"* ruling and reigning with Christ (see Gal. 6:16). One day we too will inherit the blessing of full salvation (deliverance), and our mind and body will be changed into the likeness of Jesus in the twinkle of an eye. We will have put on fully the character and power of Christ. But we must press into the prize of the high calling! The right of sonship authority is not just given to anyone. This will be given as the *prize* of our high calling by overcoming the flesh. Press on, my friend, into your high calling that is in Christ Jesus!

I see the Old Testament stories of Ishmael and Isaac and Jacob and Esau touching three different realms of time and space. First, both stories were true historical events taking place in the Middle East. Secondly, they are a spiritual snapshot of what is going on inside of every human being, especially Christians. The third one is the church at large. By this I mean that while the church is likened to a human body and also has two identities to it, an "Ishmael and Isaac." One identity is of the Spirit of God, and the other is of the flesh (devil) that is wandering in the wilderness as Ishmael lived in the wilderness all the days of his life and was married to Egypt (the world).

> And *he [Ishmael] lived in the wilderness* of Paran; and *his mother took a wife for him from the land of Egypt.* (Gen. 21:21, NASB, emphasis mine)

He lived in the wilderness of Paran, as does the rebellious church in pride. *Paran* means "the exultation of self; pride." Does this not explain the sin and rebellion that is alive in the flesh and in the harlot church? Surely living in pride and rebellion will keep us living in the wilderness where the Law of God was given. It brought sin and death to all that heard and rebelled against it. Having a traditional church mentality will keep us living in the wilderness. We will die there if we do not repent (change our mind) from our false doctrines that are stealing the truths of God from us!

We are now living in an age where the literal Ishmaelites are arising in the sinful nature of man as never before. Sin is abounding in our day. Every Arab-born child is a true Ishmaelite, and today's Moslem terrorists are Ishmael's wild sons bringing havoc to the free world and to the message of Jesus Christ. They hate the spirit of freedom that God has given us in Jesus. These are men of the Law, and their desire is to force everyone into their own beliefs, just like many Christians who want and try to force their beliefs and Laws onto others. Even though this war is going on in the world, the church, and our own flesh, *we must rejoice* because the Light will always triumph over the darkness!

> These [the beast nature] will wage war against the Lamb [within us], and *the Lamb will overcome them*, because He is Lord of lords and King of kings, and those who are with Him are the called and chosen and faithful. (Rev. 17:14, NASB, emphasis mine)

The Lamb of God will soon slay the "beast" within man with the sword of His word. We win!

Antichrist in Man
or
A Discovery of the Great Whore
That Sits Upon Many Waters

by Joseph Salmon
AD 1647

There has been much controversy about the finding out of this great whore that spirit of Antichrist, which God shall judge, and whom Christ shall destroy by the breath of His mouth, and the brightness of His coming, and in the eager pursuit of her, to find her out in her scarlet color, riding upon the beast. Some men have attained to glimmerings, some to a more perfect discovery of her, some there are that affirm this great whore to be the Pope; some the Presbyter, some the Episcopacy. Now these have seen the whore but in a fleshly discovery. *They take the fruit for the tree, the stream or the fountain. In a word, they have seen her outside, but not her inside. They know her in the History, but not in the Mystery, for upon her forehead is written,* MYSTERY BABYLON THE GREAT. (Rev. 17:5)

Know therefore, O man, whosoever you are that judges the whore by these carnal conceptions of her, that you are far deceived by her in her fleshly appearances to you.

Thus while sons of men seek to behold this strumpet in her proper sphere and center, they deceive themselves by looking too fleshly and carnally upon her. Know first then O man! That this great whore is in you. While you seek to behold her without you, while you behold her in other men, she is in the mean time acting in a Mystery in you. While you despised the appearance of her in other men, she has by guile caught you, and has stolen your heart from God and goodness. She embraces you in her arms. She kisses you with her mouth. She deceives you by her flatteries. While you think you have nothing to do with her, she is in your bosom; while you think she is far distant from you, and this is done in a Mystery and you see it not.

Now then looking upon this whore spiritually, not carnally; in us, and not out of us, in the Mystery, and not in the History; once more let us make inquisition after her, and endeavor to find her out in all her subtle and close corners. For your better attaining to the discovery of her, Consider:

First, what the great whore is.

Secondly, how she works, and what pretenses she deludes your soul by.

Thirdly, how a soul comes to attain a sight of her.

Fourthly, and last, how and when she shall be destroyed. And thus we may attain to a sight of Babylon, with her rise, and her down fall.

First, what is the Whore?

This Whore, this Babylon, this Antichrist, is your fleshly wisdom; that spiritual serpent, you are deceived by, and commit fornication with all. This wisdom of the flesh is the carnal policy of the creature.

This was that Antichrist that appeared in, and to our first parents, and that which they harlotred with from the Lord God. He created Adam blind and naked, to this end, that Adam might not see, but God for him, nor Adam might not know, but what God knew in him, and f or him. And so this Adam, though blind and naked, yet clothed with such divine robes, as were altogether inconsistent to fleshly Adam, so here was God ALL, and the creature nothing.

But now comes the serpent, which is the most subtle beast in man's worldly heart, namely, self and flesh; and that dispenses it's wisdom into the heart of the creatures, and that bids them eat, and then their eyes should be opened, and they should be as gods, knowing good and evil. Now man desiring (by the report of fleshly wisdom) to have his eyes opened, and to be as God, and to be no more a subject, but a King, no longer governed, but a Governor, runs away from God, departs from his first Lover, and commits adultery with his own fleshly wisdom. And as Adam in the History, so all in the Mystery, commit daily fornication with the whore, our fleshly wisdom, by eating of the forbidden tree. For this forbidden tree is in us, and we taste of it continually, and hourly suffer death for the same.

This Garden of Eden in the Mystery, O Man! is in you, in whom God has placed the manifestation of Himself, and has brought forth the buddings of His glory. And any of these you may eat, but there is a tree in the midst of this garden of which you may not eat, which is your heart, O man! This must be reserved wholly for the Lord; this God calls for, (Pro. 23:26).

"My son, Give me thine heart, " that is, you may ascribe nothing to yourself; but give over all man into my hands, and willingly to be no more. Then I will be in you, and to know no more than I shall know f or you, this is that forbidden tree that God would not have us eat of: but the whole man with his wisdom, reason, judgment, affections, will and understanding, must be given to the Lord. But now comes this serpent, our subtle, fleshly wisdom in us, and that thinks much to let God be all, do all, and have the glory of all: but it would fain see with it's own eyes, and be as a god unto itself. So it forsakes the rest of the trees, which God has given it to eat of, namely, the manifestation of God in the soul, and takes of its own fruit, and eats of that feast which flesh has provided, and so forsakes the fountain, and runs to the broken cistern, (Jer. 2:13). Thus our eyes come to be opened, and we see no longer light in God's light, but with the eye of self and reason, "saying to a stock, thou art my father, and to a stone, thou hast brought me forth" (Jer. 2:27) that is, attributing nothing to God, but all to fleshly wisdom, with which we have adulterated and harlotrized from the Lord.

Thus O Man! you see what that great whore is, and where she lies, even in the innermost closets of your soul. Now that you may be farther convinced that this wisdom of the flesh, is the Antichrist, the great whore, do but first consider the names, and secondly, the nature of her.

First, her names in scripture are different; as first she is called Antichrist, which is as much as to say, against Christ. Now man as a creature is not against Christ, but the wisdom in the flesh in man, this is against Christ, and so consequently the Great Whore or Antichrist.

Secondly she is called Babylon in scripture, (Rev. 17:5, 18; 2) which is as much as to say, confusion. Now all confusion that is wrought either in Pope, Presbyter, or any other particular state, is by the wisdom of the flesh, therefore this is the great Babylon.

Thirdly she is called that wicked one, (2 Thess. 3:8). Now all the actual wickedness that proceeds from the sons of men, flows from that original within, even the wisdom of the flesh. Therefore, the wisdom of the flesh is that great wicked one which is to be destroyed.

Fourthly, she is called the Mother of harlots and abominations of the earth, (Rev. 17:5). Now what is the mother of harlots? Surely this cannot be either the Pope, or any other particular state. For if the Pope be the Mother of Harlots, then I demand who or what is the Mother of his harlotry? Then what, or who, is the Mother of Harlots? Why she is in us all in a Mystery; it is the wisdom of the flesh in man, which is the mother of all the abominations which is committed against the Lord.

This is that Antichrist; this is Babylon, here is the wicked one. This is the Matron of all iniquity, out of the womb of fleshly wisdom proceeds all that actual transgression that is committed against the Lord. All outward appearances of sins, are but the bastards of this whore, the children of this strange woman, and the brats of this great adulteress. And happy, yea thrice blessed shall that Man be called, who shall take and dash these children of the whore against the stones. This man is Christ, who shall come in power and great glory in a Christian, and destroy, and dash in pieces the conceptions, bringings forth and appearances of fleshly wisdom in us, as we shall show more at large hereafter.

Thus we have endeavored to discover the whore, what she is by her names given her in scripture; whereby you may understand, that the whore does not consist by any outward state or fleshly appearances to you, but upon her fore-head, which is her most open and palpable workings, there is written Mystery.

That this great whore may yet more fully appear to be the wisdom of the flesh in you, do but consider the nature of the whore in brief. And so we have done with the first query, namely what the whore is?

Now the nature of the whore is two-fold; 1. Opposing. 2. Exalting; both which you may find attributed to Antichrist or the whore. In 2 Thess. 2:4 she opposes Christ or God and is therefore called Antichrist. Now see o Man! Whether this whore be not your fleshly wisdom. Look into your soul, and behold and see, how opposite your fleshly wisdom is to anything that is good, or goodness. What means those often resistings of the spirit in you, o Man! Do you not see how the whore deceives you? What conception, bringing forth, or appearance of God is there in you, but the wisdom of the flesh seeks to devour it, by violent attempts, and oppositions. Therefore the text says, Rev. 17:6, that the whore was drunk with the blood of the saints, and martyrs of Jesus. How has this mystical whore, the wisdom of the flesh, martyred the appearance of Christ in you, so that indeed she is drunk with the blood of many a sanctified motion of the spirit in you? The wisdom of the flesh is that mystical Saul that hunts after the blood of David, which is, the tender appearance of God in the soul. This is what crucifies the Lamb afresh, and puts him to open shame. And all this is done by that bloody whore that harbors in your bosom.

The wisdom of the flesh is that bond-slave that always resents wisdom's children, and the children of the free women, which are the bringings forth of Jesus in you. In a word, this is that great red Dragon, spoken of in Rev. 12:3–4 who stands before the women, which is, a Christian under the pangs of new birth, ready to be delivered oh the blesses child Jesus, in whose heart God is begetting Himself, in His own form and image. This I say is that dragon, even the wisdom of the flesh, which is ready to devour the sweet Babe, even Jesus, with His form and feature in the soul, and endeavors to make it an abortive. This is that mystical Herod that seeks the ruin of the appearance of God in our flesh and thus you see what the opposing nature of the whore is, who f or her bloody opposition against the manifestation of God in His people, shall have blood to drink, when she shall be found worthy.

We now proceed to the other qualification of the nature of this whore, which is a high, proud, lofty, aspiring nature, being manifested by two things.

1. In that she will get into God's Temple (2 Thess. 2:4). In that she will therein exalt herself above all that is called God, and she will be a god to herself. Behold O man (as it were in

a glass) the true physiognomy and perfect portraiture of your fleshly wisdom.

First then, consider that your heart is that temple of God, where this great whore sits. Therefore mind the apostle, 1 Cor. 3:16, "Know ye not that ye are the temple of God," also chap. 6:19. Now you being this temple of God, your fleshly wisdom is that Antichrist, that whore that sits in your heart. You are that beast that this whore rides upon, Rev. 17:3. For the Psalmist says in Psalm 49:12 that man being in honor abideth not, but is like the beast that perisheth. Here you may see, O man! the Pride of the wisdom of the flesh that no place will serve her, but God's temple the heart of man, that God has set apart for the praise of his glory, does this whore make her beast, by bringing it to be subject to her dominion; this temple of God to be that den of thievery, which God has made for his own honor and dignity.

Secondly, the exalting nature of the whore is seen, not only by her climbing up into God's Temple, and so becomes that Lucifer, that fell down to hell. But also by her behavior in God's Temple, she exalts herself above all that is called God, and she sits as God in God's Temple, in a place where she has no right to rule and govern.

Behold here, O Christian! another proper emblem of the flesh in you. How this whore, this mystical Babylon, does exalt herself above every appearance of God in you: inasmuch as her tail draws a third of the stars of heaven, and casts them down to the earth, which is in me? That reason, will, affections and judgement, which are as the civil powers and lights of the soul, all these are drawn after this beast; so that indeed, she now is the Lady of the Kingdom (Isa. 47:7) nay vs. 8 "I am and there is none else beside me." This wisdom of the flesh is that which will not allow the child Jesus any room in the Inn of your heart, but thrusts him into the manger, which is, under the meanest thoughts, poorest respects, and lowest Love of your soul. But in the mean time this whore herself takes the largest rooms, and highest chambers, that is, she is most supreme in your affections; with the greatest honor and respect that may be. Thus does this whore, the wisdom of the flesh, exalt herself as God; yea and that in God's Temple, where she has no right to rule and govern. For the Apostle tells us that we are not our own, but we are bought with a price. That is, we are to own no Lord, but He that has bought us; to render no obedience or servitude to any, but to that God who in our flesh has redeemed us according to the commandment, "Thou shalt have no other gods before me." But self, flesh, and creature, would be God in God's Kingdom, which causes God to take up a complaint against his people of old. "Have I been a barren wilderness to thee, or a land of darkness, wherefore then say my people, we are lords, and we will come no more after thee." (Jer. 2:31)

Now the creature running away from the lord, commits fornication with the great whore, the wisdom of the flesh; attributing all power, glory, salvation, and happiness to selfish wisdom. And therefore Babylon says on this wise, Isa. 14:13, "I will ascend into heaven; I will exalt my throne above the stars of God," which is when the wisdom of the flesh is exalted above the highest sphere of divine light in the soul, nay vs. 14, "I will be like the most high."

Behold, O man! The aspiring, exalting nature of your carnal wisdom. The wisdom of the serpent would have Adam to be as God, and to see by his own eyes, and to walk with his own light, which serpent is nothing in the Mystery but the wisdom of the flesh, carrying the soul above that center which God has seated it in; causing you to walk by her blaze, and not in God's light to 'see light; to hate, scorn, and put a mean elimination upon any motion of God or goodness; always thinking your way is best, and your counsel safest. And thus does this whore your fleshly wisdom, exalt herself above all that is called God in you; and sits as God in your soul, which is God's Temple. So much f or the answer to the first question; namely what this great whore is?

Now you having attained some spiritual discovery of this whore, both by her names and nature; it remains, that we proceed in answer to the second question: which is namely, how this whore works, and what pretenses she deludes your soul by.

Now therefore know, O Man! That this whore works in a Mystery. Upon her forehead is written, "MYSTERY." Rev. 17.

When Antichrist, or your fleshly wisdom is most apparent in any sinful action, yet in that appearance she is very mystical: so that indeed, upon her most open workings in the heart, there is written "MYSTERY."

It is a property of a strumpet to pretend what she does not intend to her lovers. Behold a character of the Mother of Harlots, your fleshly wisdom: she is very subtle of heart. Pro.

7. She always pretends what she never intends, so that here all is well in the History, but all is mere deceit and delusion in the Mystery. This whore, she will present a glorious show, but there is nothing but wickedness and harlotry intended.

This is that spiritual Judas that will betray you with his salutations. You shall find this whore in a religious dress, many times; that hereby she may deceive the heart of the simple. Observe how the harlot in Prov. 7 beguiled the young man. "She caught him, and kissed him," **vs.** 13, "and with an impudent face, she said unto him: I have peace offerings with me, this day have I paid my vows." This whore in the Mystery, is your fleshly wisdom, and you are this simple young man, who are deluded by her. Behold therefore, O Man! The impudency and boldness of this spiritual whore; she is not ashamed to show her forehead to you. But here is a Mystery all this while that you see it not.

Now therefore know, O Christian! That this whore appears to you in all your spiritual performances, and sacrifices to the Lord. If then you but observe, you shall see her appear in prayer, in humiliation, in fasting, nay, in all outward ordinances, you shall see your wisdom in all these things, steal your heart from the Lord, by attributing something to form, flesh and creature: so that *we are apt oftentimes to bless ourselves in our spiritual performances, and sing a requiem to ourselves in our fleshly forms*; so that hereby, all our duties are but the sacrifices of the whore, the vows of our fleshly wisdom which she appear in, to delude us.

Now, woe and alas f or us! That we should ever be deceived by this whore, in those things wherein we think she appears least, herein is plainly seen her mystical apparition.

This whore meets you, O Man, in all your religious performances; and there does she attribute all the goodness of all that is done, to her self. And you also gave consent to it, and to commit fornication with her. Hence it is that the woman is said, (Rev. 17), to have a golden cup in her hand, full of abominations, and filthiness of her fornications, a golden pot, but a bitter potion.

This serpent, our fleshly wisdom appears to us with her speckled skin, but within her there is deadly poison. Beware then of this whore, in all her glorious appearances, and golden manifestations, for all this is but to ensnare your heart with her treachery. The wisdom of the flesh will meet you many times arrayed in purple and scarlet, colored and decked with gold; which in the Mystery are nothing else but shews of glory to you. She will meet you in good performances; and there she will salute you, and tell you that your good duties have prevailed with God for you; and she will tell you that because you are under such an outward form and carnal dispensation that therefore you are better than other Christians, which enjoy God in a more spiritual making out of himself. Thus she will endeavor to make you drink of her fornications, by proposing her golden cup to you: and thus poor seduced man, commits folly with himself; or his own wisdom in all outward worship whatsoever, forsakes God, in praying, fasting, mourning, and all outward forms; and is carried away more with the decency, order, and trimness of the whore, in an outward dispensation, than the power and life of Godliness, that God requires in a Christian. And so much shall suffice for the setting forth of the first delusive pretense of the whore, which is to array herself in her glory, the better to effect her design upon the poor creature.

2. The design of Antichrist, or your fleshly wisdom, is always to bring you out of love with God. It is death to the whore, when she sees that you desire to be constant to your husband Jesus, who has espoused you to Himself; and therefore she is still laboring to bring you out of love with Christ, and God.

And this she labors to effect, by causing you to think that God does not love you, that hereby she might estrange your heart from the Lord.

It is the work of the serpent, to raise in our hearts, hard thoughts of God. All poor afflicted souls, whoever you are that grieve under the pangs of an accusing conscience, hearken, behold and consider! How the wisdom of the flesh deludes you, by causing you to look upon God in the glass of flesh and creature; and so hereby apprehend Him to be what He is not!

Poor soul I you tell me there is no mercy in a Christ f or you, and I pray thee why so? O, alas! God loves me not, He is offended at me, and displeased with me; I have been so vile a sinner against Him.

Now all this while the poor soul does but look upon God according to the dictates of selfish wisdom. And so it apprehends God to be like itself: "Thou thoughtest," saith God, "that I had been altogether such a one as thyself." Because we are angry with

God many times, therefore we are apt to think God is froward with us; whereas, God is love, says the apostle, Eph. 1:4, 2:4. And therefore God tells us that His thoughts are not our thoughts, nor our ways, His ways, Is. 55:8.

The wisdom of the flesh endeavors to put out, and extinguish the light of God in a Christian, whereby the soul might see God to be purely Love and Mercy; and will propose its own glass to the creature; which renders God to be what He is not, to man's apprehension.

So that when the soul would fain be refreshed with the comfortable aspect of God's presence, then comes fleshly wisdom, and tells the soul it must not behold God according to His Love, but according to its own iniquity and so hereby, dashes the soul upon the rock of desperation; insomuch that the poor creature now concludes that God is angry with him, and is resolved not to show him mercy.

Now when the whore has thus estranged the heart from the Lord, by persuading the soul, that either God is not able, or willing to help in its misery; then she propounds her own way to the creature; she will persuade the creature never to go to God again; but rather with the prodigal, to go and feed upon the husks: as namely, upon prayer, fasting, or some outward and carnal ordinances. And here the soul estranged from the substance, commits adultery with the whore, in subsisting on the shadow, forsaking the fountain, running to the broken cisterns, and so commits a great evil against the Lord. And thus poor naked man runs from God, as from an enemy, behind the trees of his own creating; and before he will be beholding to God for clothing, he will cover himself with the fig-leaves of his own fleshly wisdom, and so commits adultery with the Mother of Harlots. And now you see another delusive pretense of the whore raining hard thoughts of God in you, by bringing you out of love with the Lord your Husband, so that she might the better steal your heart from God, and rob Him of His due and propriety.

3. This Mother of Harlots, your fleshly wisdom will propose herself to be all to you, so that she may draw all your action after her. She will tell you that she can supply all your wants, and relieve your necessities, and therefore you need not to be beholden to God f or anything. She will tell you with Adam that she can give you the knowledge of good and evil, and she can open your eyes and she it is that gives you anything. Therefore the text says, Prov. 9:13, "A foolish woman is clamorous: she is simple, and knoweth nothing." This foolish woman is your fleshly wisdom, O Man! For the Apostle says, the wisdom of the flesh is foolishness with the Lord; which although it be foolish, simple and knows nothing, yet she is very clamorous; that is, her voice must chiefly be harkened unto. If the still, small voice of the Spirit utter itself in your soul, how does the clamor of your foolish fleshly wisdom as it were out-cry, and drown the utterings of God in you. Therefore the text says, vs. 14, that "she sits in the door of her house, and the highest places of the city, to call passengers who go right on their ways; whoso is simple let him turn in hither, and as f or him that wanteth understanding,

she saith, stolen waters are sweet, and bread eaten in secret is pleasant."

Alas! Poor seduced man that reads this history, and sees not that you yourself are the very person intended. Know therefore that you are this passenger, who while you are traveling right on the way to seek after Christ, are deluded by the clamor of this strange woman. While you are seeking after wisdom, she bids you turn in hither. She has wisdom and knowledge for you, although she is simple and knows nothing. O sirs! How wise would self be, when it is nothing but folly in the abstract.

And thus, O Man! You are invited to Babylon's banquet, and run after the stolen waters of the whore, your fleshly wisdom; which stolen waters in the Mystery, are nothing else but the depriving of God of His due in all His works in the soul. When God brings forth His wisdom and divine light in the soul, then flesh and self will tell you that all proceeds from them, and so steal God's propriety from Him. And thus man runs from God, and is estranged from the Lord, and eats bread secretly from the harlot.

And this (in my apprehension) is a third delusive pretence of the whore, so to show herself to the creature as if all fullness were treasured in her; in whom indeed is nothing but vacancy and emptiness. Thus does this whore draw us from the Lord our Lover, who has ever been constant to us, and that in the very height of our inconsistency to him.

It is the design of God in us, to bring us to live upon His fulness, and to feed upon those divine dainties, which He will carve out to us. And what soul is it that in the time of his constancy to the Lord, ever wanted anything? Nay what Spiritual refreshments and incomes of divine glory have our souls tasted of, while we have kept in our Father's house?

But when Jeshurun waxes fat, and kicks (Deut. 32: 15); when once we, prodigal-like forsake our Father, and think that there is enough in self and creature to subsist upon; when once we begin to loathe the heavenly manna, Christ Jesus, and to esteem more of the fleshpots, garlic and onions of Egypt, the raw and rank discovery of this whore of bondage in us, when we prefer the husks of swinish self, and wisdom before the dainties of our Father's table; truly we at last come to know the want of divine joy and comfort.

Know therefore, O Man! that in all your wanderings from the Lord your full fountain, to self, your broken cistern; you in the mean time, are drawn by the whore of your fleshly wisdom, to yield to her wickedness, by her flattering lips she forces you, Prov. 7:21, and you go after her as a silly ox to the slaughter, till a dart strike through your liver; which darts is one of the fiery darts, which the apostle speaks of, even the woundings of the conscience, the gnawings of the worm in you. And this is that spiritual death, which you have brought upon yourself, by committing adultery with the

whore, your fleshly wisdom; who has stolen your heart from the Lord, by attributing all fullness to herself in you. And now she leaves you, as not being able to help you in your woe, distress and misery. And so much shall suffice for the discovery of a third delusive pretense of the whore, whereby she deceives the heart of the simple man.

4. This whore, the wisdom of the flesh, is very changeable in her appearances. It is the policy of an harlot to suit herself to the humor and fancy of her lovers, so thereby she may still retain and keep them in her favor.

Even so it is with the spiritual whore, the Mother of Harlots, your fleshly wisdom, which will still be moving and changing herself in her appearances to you, so that her design may be carried on the more subtly. Therefore the text says, Prov. 5:6, "Lest thou shouldest ponder the path of life, her ways are moveable, thou canst not know them. "Behold here, as in a glass, the nature of this whorish woman, the wisdom of the flesh! How moveable she is in all the puttings forth of her self to man. If your heart leads you to all manner of palpable profanities this whore will encourage you to this course of life, and she will tell you, that there is time enough yet to be sorry for your misdeeds, and if through the motions of goodness, you begin to ponder of your wickedness; and therefore are resolved to mend your wicked courses and to be more virtuous f or the time to come; this whore will move with you hither also. She will lead you forth to the presence of many a good moral action, as to extend alms, to feed the hungry, to clothe the naked, to visit the sick, and to leave your old vices you have formerly lived in. All this she will be well contented with. She will be willing with Saul, to kill part of the spoil, some open vices and palpable profanities; but Agag, and the fattest of the cattle, the chief lusts of your heart, she will work yet under; that in the Mystery must be spared. (I Sam. 15:9) Thus will the whore conform herself to man; nay, if you are brought by higher light to see that Godliness does not consist only in refraining from some open vices, and embracing their contrary virtues; but there must be religion, as well as morality looked after. And there-fore now you are resolved to take upon you some outward profession of Christianity.

This whore will change her appearances to you here also. She will come forth to meet you with her peace offering and her vows. She will move you to fasting, prayer, and humiliation, provided, that all this while you attribute the glory of all to herself. She will move as high as any outward ordinance with you, *and all this is lest you should ponder the path of life.*

Lest you should question this whore in her wanton gesture, and gaudy attire, she will behave herself more religiously, and adorn herself more demurely; so that hereby she may the more cunningly draw your affections after her, and thus poor seduced man is mystically misled, by the flatteries of this whorish woman. In the mean time he thinks he serves God. And this is a 4th pretense of the Mother of Harlots, to move and change in all her appearances to you, so that by her conformity to you in every respect, she may keep your affections entirely to herself.

5. It is the property of this strange woman,' your fleshly wisdom, to render Christ to be at a distance from you, in all her fornications with you.

If man in all his adulteries from the Lord, did but seriously consider and really understand, that his first lover Christ Jesus is in him, and sees him in all his strayings from Him; and how he eats his bread secretly, with the wisdom of the flesh; surely he would be ashamed of his folly, And would not dare thus to commit harlotry in the light of his spiritual Lover. And this the wisdom of the flesh knows right well, and therefore labors might and main to render Christ at a distance from the creature, so that the soul might not be afraid to commit fornication with her.

Therefore it is the language of the whore, Prov. 7:19–20. The good man is not at home, he is gone into a far country. And behold the language of this mystical strumpet, the wisdom of the flesh! She will persuade you that you may take a little liberty to sin that you may exalt self a little, in religious performances, for God sees you not. He is in heaven, and not in your heart; and thus, man being deluded by this whore, becomes that fool who said in his heart, "there is no God, "so that he might magnify, deify and worship self in God's stead.

Self and flesh will not own the manifestation of God in the soul, when the Lord lets forth the beams of His glory into the heart of man, and does, as it were, draw up the soul to a higher center, by giving it some taste of the powers of the world to come: it is the work of your fleshly wisdom to extinguish this divine light in the soul, and as it were to corrupt the stomach, and put the mouth out of taste, so that it might not relish or digest those divine dainties.

And notwithstanding those open appearances of Christ in you, yet the wisdom of the flesh will tell you, that the good man Christ Jesus is gone abroad; He is at a distance from you. This whore will be contented that you should know anything but Christ Jesus, and Him crucified in you. She is willing that you should know Christ naturally, but not spiritually; Christ in the History, but not in the Mystery: Christ for you, but not Christ in you. It is possible f or a man to know very much of the flesh of Christ, to be acquainted with the History of Godliness, to live under carnal ordinances and fleshly dispensations, to talk and dispute upon high principles, to be higher in the understanding of scriptures than others, by the head and shoulders with Saul; and yet f or all this, he may in all these things commit adultery with the whore. All these things may be to him no more, than the sacrifices and the vows of this spiritual whore, the wisdom of the flesh. He is not the true Professor therefore, that can read, hear, fast and pray, and worship God in outward dispensation; but those are the true circumcision that worship God in the Spirit, and rejoice in Christ Jesus, and have no confidence in the flesh:

He is not a Christian indeed that does by the power of nature, believe what is naturally and historically reported of Christ in ' the scripture but he that by the power of the Spirit, believes all this History to be verified in him in the Mystery. For there is a History, and a Mystery of Christ. The History is, Christ for us, *the Mystery is, Christ in us*. Col. 1:27.

Now that power of nature which is implanted in man, is sufficient for giving credit to whatsoever Christ is, or has been f or us, but not f or what Christ is in us. This must be a power equal with that which raised up Jesus from the dead, Eph. 1:20.

Your fleshly wisdom will be contented that you should be acquainted with what Christ has done for you, but she will not endure to let you see Him in you.

First, she is willing to let you understand that Christ has been made flesh for you, but not that the Word is made flesh in you; that is, that *God by His own power has begotten Himself, and brought forth Himself in His own likeness in you*; that you are this virgin that is over-shadowed with power from on high; *and have the immortal seed of God in you, which immortal seed by its own power, brings forth its own self in your soul*, by the puttings forth of the motions of the Spirit in you. This your fleshly wisdom will not let you behold. The wisdom of the flesh is that serpent, Rev. 12:15, that casts out the flood after the woman, or a Christian, in whom Christ is by the power of the Spirit born and brought forth. This flood in the Mystery is, nothing in me but the overflowing of the wisdom of the flesh, and the inundation's of sinful flesh and creature, that flow into the heart of man; this spiritual serpent, hereby endeavoring to drown and destroy, both Christ and a Christian, at once as it were, both the passive Mother, and the active. babe suddenly, such an enemy is the wisdom of the flesh to Christ in us.

This flood of iniquity, these over-flowings of the wisdom of the flesh in us, is that great river Euphrates, that must be dried up, that way be made for the King of the East, Christ Jesus, to ruin great Babel in man's heart. And thus you see briefly, how the wisdom of the flesh is an enemy to Christ born in us.

2. She cannot endure to let us see the dying of this Christ in us, although we are the very persons that crucifies the Lamb afresh, and puts Him to open shame. Yet she will persuade us otherwise; and thus poor self-seduced man, crucifies his Savior every day afresh; and yet is so deluded by himself, that he sees it not.

Consider then, O man, that you are this spiritual Jerusalem, where Christ is slain. You are that judge that condemns Christ in the motions of His Spirit, and lets Barabbas, or your base lust, go uncontrolled: all the faculties of your soul, and the powers of the inner man, misled by the wisdom of the flesh, as it were the voice of the people, crucify Him, crucify Him." Your sins are those spears that pierce Christ in spirit, in you. And thus, O man, you are the daily cross of your Savior. And how happy you should be if you discern all this, so that you might look upon Him whom you now pierce, and mourn for your iniquity: but the design of this whore, your fleshly wisdom, is to darken your eye from beholding this. She will rather tell you that the good man is not at home, Christ is not in you in His sufferings.

And thus poor man, misled by the whore, becomes that deceitful Pilate, that washes his hands of the blood of this innocent spirit, whom it has despitefully crucified.

But secondly, Christ may be said to die in a Christian another way, which also this whore cannot endure we should see and behold; that is, when Christ dies in flesh to us, and in us; f or sometimes Christ lives in fleshly appearances of Himself in a Christian. Some Christians, the highest discovery of Christ that they have attained unto, is fleshly forms and fleshly ordinances; and thus many a Christian enjoys Christ as really and as comfortably, as the disciples did th4 natural flesh of Christ. Now Christ would need to die, depart, go away from His disciples in the flesh, so that He might come in a higher, and more glorious dispensation to them. Even so Christ does of ten times die in a Christian, to all outward and fleshly dispensations, and this death the wisdom of the flesh cannot endure that the soul should discern. How often does God go out of all low appearances to a Christian? Insomuch that a poor Christian can many times find no life in the forms, no comfort in the ordinances, no joy in duties and performances; but with Mary, stands weeping at the sepulchre, or those dead dispensations where Christ is buried, and can see no more appearance of Jesus in them, but all this while it seeks the living among the dead: and thus Christ dies in a Christian to all fleshly appearances, many times. And truly, look what sorrow fell upon the spirits of the poor disciples, for the departure of their Lord (in the flesh) from them; the like sorrow and grief falls upon that Christian, from whom Christ is departed in all outward dispensations.

Christ compares that present estate and condition of the disciples to a woman in travail, Jo. 16:21–22. And ye now therefore have sorrow, says Christ: Behold O Christian; the lively image of our condition! when Christ crucifies His own flesh to us, in all those outward dispensations, wherein we have formerly enjoyed God.

Happily, heretofore we have seen much of God in our outward formal fellowships one with another, in fleshly ordinances; as baptism of water, and breaking of bread; but now happily Christ is crucified in all these things to us, and we find nothing but dead flesh there; nothing that can administer any spiritual comfort in any of these things; see nothing but form and bare flesh, bare water, bare bread, and wine; insomuch that we now confess, that our highest attainment of the knowledge of Christ, has been but a knowledge after the flesh, now here lies Christ crucified to all these things, and the soul dead to its wonted discoveries.

Now the design of your fleshly wisdom, is to darken this death of Christ in you. She cannot endure that the soul should move out of its fleshly discoveries; for she loves the outward order, and fleshly decency of all these things. Therefore she'll tell you that Christ must be found here, or no where; and thus keeps the soul in bondage to herself; insomuch that the poor creature goes again and again to his outward worship, and yet finds no living Christ there; nor is possessed with any more comfort in them, than proceeds from the power of the flesh, whereas indeed the soul should be willing to wait in this dead condition; for the return of the Spirit; to lie empty and bare at the gate of mercy, out of all those formal dispensations, from whence Christ is departed; waiting for the Comforter. Therefore my counsel is to all those who see Christ dead to all such carnal and fleshly dispensations in them: Christian, wait upon the Lord, and you shall renew your strength. Christ must have His time to lie in the grave, hidden from you in all His appearances to you; but this know, He will see you again, in a more spiritual discovery of Himself. It is but a while, and He that shall come will come, and will not tarry; and will take you up into Himself, above those types and figures. He will be your water, and bread, and wine to you. *He will bring you to the enjoyment of the substance, and you shall no more live upon the shadow. You shall live upon the kernel, and not always be cracking upon the shell.* For if we be dead with Christ, we shall also live together with Him. But be sure in the mean time that you beware of the whore, lest by her appearances to you in all outward worship, make you believe that Christ is living in all those things wherein He is dead and buried. And thus in brief, you see that this strumpet, the wisdom of the flesh, is an enemy to the discovery of Jesus Christ in us. And now me thinks by this time we may see who is the great Antichrist that John speaks of in his first epistle, I Jo. 4:3. That every spirit that believes not, or denies Christ come in the flesh, is Antichrist: And what is it now that denies Christ come in the flesh? If you would know Christian what this Antichrist is, and where she lies, you need not go far to discover it; you need not go to Rome, Canterbury, or Westminster, but you may find that Antichrist in you, denying Jesus to be come in the flesh.

Oh, all you that would fain show yourselves professed enemies to this Antichrist, that man of sin, who seeks to destroy root and branch, all those in whom you conceive there are appearances of Him. Return, return O man, into your own bosom, and there behold him lying secretly in your own soul. There is the Antichrist that denies every manifestation of God in your flesh.

This is the whore that you commit fornication with daily. This is the Babylon, whose downfall will be joyous to the saints. This is the heretic and the schismatic. This it is that makes rents and divisions among us: and therefore we ought everyone of us, to desire God to subdue the wisdom of the flesh in us, and to wait upon the Lord until He comes to show us the judgment of the spiritual whore, this Antichrist in us; and not so much desire downfall of either Pope, Presbyter, or Independent, or any other state whatsoever; but to desire the ruin of this mystical Babylon, which is the Mother of all our harlotry from the Lord. And so, much will suffice f or answer to the second question, which is namely: How the whore works, and what pretenses she deludes the soul by?

We proceed now in order to a third question. Namely, 3. How the soul comes to attain to a sight of her? In which we shall first propose the way that God does usually take to discover this whore to a Christian.

Second, when the soul sees her, how and in what manner it apprehends her.

First, for the way that a soul comes to attain a sight of her by.

If then, you would know the way how a Christian comes to a spiritual sight of flesh and self; know, that God must deal with you as He did with John, Rev. 17. When God would show John the judgment of the great whore, and give him a discovery of the whore, he takes him, vs. 3, and carried him away in the Spirit into the wilderness, and then says John, I saw a woman, etc.

First then know that you can never behold self aright, till God take you up, or carry you away in the Spirit. The spiritual man, says the apostle, seeth all things, discovers all things, and judgeth all things. So much as the Lord spiritualizes a Christian, so much he sees into himself, and discerns and beholds this mystical whore the wisdom of the flesh, in himself: and how he judges and esteems of her as that whore, that adulteress with whom he has (in all his ways and worships) adulterated from the Lord.

Therefore the Apostle says that the spirit searcheth all things, 1 Cor. 2: 10. So long as the soul lies under the veil of the flesh, so long self is undiscovered to him. For while the creature lies wrapped up in the mantle of nature, it is in a spiritual slumber of sleep: and lies as one passive, under the workings of the wisdom of the flesh; rocked asleep in the cradle of fleshly security. But now when God speaks by the still, small voice, and yet powerful utterance of the Spirit in a Christian, "Come up hither," when God takes a soul beyond self and creature; insomuch that now the creature sees all but vanity below Christ: now I say, the creature comes to some discovery of himself, but never before.

That man that will view the breadth and length of a city at once, must not always be walking around in the streets; but he must assay to get up to the top of some mountain that lies above it, and so the city shall be discovered to him, with its breadth and length. Even so it is with the spiritual Babel, which is in you, O Man! even the wisdom of the flesh. You must be taken above it, before you can truly and really discover it.

2. You must be carried away in the Spirit; carried quite away from all power, policy, strength, motion and action of the creature.

3. The place where you must be carried into is a wilderness, which is into a lost condition to sin and self. Never does the soul attain to a real sight of the flesh, till the Lord by His Spirit does (as it were) lose the soul to itself . When the creature comes to be at a loss in itself, in all its fleshly performances, not knowing where to have recourse, but sees that his narrow fleshly heart is so wide a wilderness that he is lost in the many turnings and windings thereof; now the creature comes to behold his spiritual adulteries; now he sees to what a lost condition he is fallen; and how the whore all this while in all his duties, worships, forms and disciplines, has stolen his heart from the Lord, his first lover and tender husband. Paul was carried away by the Spirit into this wilderness, Phil. 3:7–9, he professes in verse 7, that what things were gain to him, he counted loss for Christ. "Yea doubtless, " he says vs. 8, "And I count all things but loss f or the excellency of Christ Jesus my Lord, for whom I have suffered the loss of all -things, and do count them but dung, that I may win Christ." Paul never knew himself, nor creature, excellency aright, till God showed him the excellency of the knowledge of Christ. And when, he comes to see the worth of Christ, then he sees himself in a wilderness. In this wilderness or lost condition, he spies the vanity of all that was flesh below Christ; so that now when God carries away a soul in the Spirit, and lopes it as it were, to itself , and lets loose the beams of his own glory upon it,

ravishes the heart with his own beauty, catches him up as it were to the third heavens, and shows such divine excellency as it never yet apprehended, the soul by the clear aspect of his beautifical vision of God, begins now to see the vanity and deformity of itself, and is (as it were) in as great amazement of spirit, as the man doubtless was, who was born blind from the womb, and yet now comes to see the sun, or as one that has been shut up in a dark dungeon, and now comes to walk in the light. Even thus is it with poor man in the highest glory and excellency of the flesh. When God sends forth the beams of that Sun of Righteousness upon poor man, how dark he beholds himself to be, as he stands in relation to all fleshly excellency, when God shows him the worth, value and excellency of himself in Christ; what loss, dung and dross does a Christian esteem those things to be, though formerly never so glorious and excellent; and therefore Paul now no longer desires to be found in his own excellency, or in himself, but he says, vs. 9, "that I may be found in him, not having my own righteousness, which is of the law, but that which is through the faith of Christ." The light of Christ's excellency, it does so fully discover self and flesh to the Christian, as that now he loathes the scarlet color, the glorious attire of the whore, even all its golden performances, her gilded vows and sacrifices.

O, all you poor souls, who are apt to place your glory in anything below Christ, and to hang your righteousness upon your prayers, fastings, mournings or any outward ordinances, alas how far you are mistaken! Who when the Lord comes to carry you away in the Spirit, to see all your glory in Christ, your righteousness in Him; you will then see the odiousness of everything below Christ, which you have wondered after. You will then desire that God might find you in this wilderness, quite out of self; that there may not be any hoof of the beast in you, but that you may be wholly incorporated into Christ: in whom you now see your glory to consist. And thus you see what the way is that God uses to discover self, or this whore the wisdom of the flesh, to the soul.

Secondly, let us consider how and in what manner the soul beholds the whore.

A poor creature whom the Lord has carried away, or taken up into the Spirit, that now lives and walks in the Spirit, he sees and beholds himself not as he was wont to do formerly. Happily you were wont to see a glory and excellency in things that were below God, but now on the contrary how loathsome is everything, that comes short of the divine excellency of Christ. Happily heretofore you have seen some worth in your prayers, and in your tears, but now you see all these things which before were counted gain, to be but loss unto you. You behold all your own righteousness to be but a menstruous cloth, and as a filthy rag. Happily heretofore you boasted of your pedigree with Paul; of the tribe of Benjamin, and of the stock of Israel; that you are descended from such a reformed church, from such visible dispensations; so that as touching all legal worship, outward forms, and ordinances, you may be nominated a Pharisee. But now you see the lowness, and weakness of these fleshly things, wherein you have formerly boasted. Now you rejoice that you have attained to the knowledge of that Christ which is the end or substance of all these fleshly things unto you, so that now you have no confidence in the flesh any longer; but are become one of the true circumcision that worship God in the Spirit, and rejoices in Christ Jesus. In a word, this spiritualized Christian, sees all below Christ to be but the garment of this spiritual strumpet, that she uses to appear in to deceive him. He now sees the whore, and her various pretenses, and how she has formerly deceived him in her several dresses; he sees her not only in her gaudy attire, but in the height of her modesty, even in her religious garment, so that now he sees how the wisdom of the flesh makes use of all outward worship, forms and ordinances, to deceive the heart of the simple.

Finally, this spiritual man, has the same discovery of this whorish wisdom, as John had, Rev. 17, vs. 3–7.

1. John saw the woman sitting upon a scarlet colored beast. Truly when God carries you away in the Spirit, you will behold yourself to be the beast, that this mystical whore, the wisdom of the flesh, does thus enslave man in his fallen condition from God; as it were Satan's pack horse to act all his designs of wickedness.

This beast had seven heads and ten horns. These seven heads and ten horns are seven mountains and ten kings, the scripture says; which in me are nothing but those powers of man which God has endued him with all; as reason, will, affection, understanding and the like; and all these (vs. 13) do with one consent give and ascribe their power to the beast, or poor bestialized man. And this beast man, employs all these with their power to make war against the Lamb Christ Jesus, vs. 14. And so here is a discovery of poor misled man, fighting the battle of the whore, his fleshly wisdom. All this does the Christian apprehend in himself, when the Lord carries him away in the Spirit of His glory.

2. John saw the woman, vs. 4, arrayed in purple and scarlet color, decked with gold, pearls and precious stones. Truly Christian, when the Lord takes away this false glassy eye of the flesh from you, and endues you with spiritual eye-sight from Himself, you shall see this whore, your fleshly wisdom, in all this her glory and excellency in you. For all these golden pearls and precious stones, and scarlet colors, are but the trimmings of the whore, that she usually puts on and clothes herself with all, when she comes out to meet the sons of men; so that hereby she might with the more facility dazzle the eyes, infatuate and bewitch the senses of her spiritual lovers. But now when God takes up a soul into Spirit, then flesh is, as it were, unclothed to the creature. Now the soul looks not at her glorious shows, which formerly had bewitched his heart; but he sees and knows that under that golden habit, there walks this subtle harlot. Under this speckled skin, there is a venomous, viperous, serpentine carcass. The man whom God has spiritualized, when the wisdom of the flesh appears in him in her glory, clad with excellency, and adorned with all her beautiful robes; yet all this while he sees her naked and bare: the Spirit teaches him to look inwardly, and not altogether outwardly; and this is such a Mystery, that the poor carnal heart cannot discern, because he looks fleshly and carnally, and has not yet received this spiritual eyesight from above.

3. But then, John saw the woman having a golden cup in her hand, full of abominations and filthiness of her fornications.

Now the soul which God wraps up in that spirit of glory, he beholds this whore in him, and sees how she has deluded him by her golden cup, to taste of the wine of her fornications. For this golden cup in the whore's hand, is (in the Mystery of it) the gilded pretenses, and golden appearances of the wisdom of the flesh; in which pretenses there is contained, the wickedness of her abominations, and filthiness of her fornication.

A man caught up, and carried by the Spirit to walk in the life of Christ, and to live in the purity of God, sees himself (as it were) now awakened out of the drunken sleep of the whore, newly risen out of the defiled bed of the flesh; from the spiritual vomits, swinish abominations, and beastly uncleanness that he before wallowed in.

4. Again John saw, vs. 5, what was written upon the woman is forehead.

Truly, until such time as the Lord takes a soul up into Spirit, though the wisdom of the flesh appear openly to him, though she shows her very forehead, yet he cannot discern her in her appearances. But now when God has caught the soul into Spirit, and carried him away in the Spirit, then he sees the whore in her apparitions. He beholds Mystery in the forehead, or palpable workings of the whore; Mystery in all her specious pretenses: and notwithstanding all her shows of glory. Yet he sees she is indeed and in truth Babylon the great: the great confused whore, which breeds all that confusion of spirit in a Christian; and all that commotion, disturbance, and out-cries that are in the heart of man, all those heavy, sad and disconsolate thoughts that man is possessed with all; all that disorder that many a time is in the soul; every hard thought of God; every despairing imagination; all the gnawings of conscience in the creature. So that (I say) he now sees her to be the great Babel, or confused whore, who is the Mother of Harlots and abominations of the earth.

5. But then lastly, John saw the woman drunk with the blood of the saints and martyrs of Jesus.

Truly this is the very physiognomy and portraiture of the whore. To a Christian that is carried away in the Spirit, he now comes to behold her a drunken, blood thirsty whore. He now sees how the whore has martyred the bringings forth of Christ, slain and crucified that man Jesus afresh. He sees how the whore is drunk with the blood of the Lamb in him. In a word, the saints truly spiritualized, beholds self and flesh to be the most hateful, detestable, loathsome thing in the world to him. Look how loathsome and injurious a man's vomit is to his stomach, even so loathsome is self to that Christian, from whose stomach God has fetched up all the corrupt flesh, by bringing the soul to be lovesick of Christ, with the operative pills of His blessed Spirit. O, how hateful now is the golden cup and sweet wine of the whore, to a spiritualized man; insomuch that he now loathes and abhors himself in dust and ashes. Nay he begins now to wonder at himself , in his own shame and folly, as the text says, vs. 6, that when John saw the whore he wondered with great admiration. Truly, the same is the condition of every Christian, who by the carryings away by the Spirit, comes to a spiritual sight of this whore, the wisdom of the flesh, he now wonders that he should be drawn to commit folly by so filthy an harlot. He now wonders that such a bulk of filthiness, such a mountain of wickedness, and spring of bitterness should be in him, and he never till now was able to discern it. He now wonders that ever the lenity and mercy of God should so long bear with him in all his adulteries with this swinish whore. He now wonders that God at. last has brought him to such a sight and discovery; he admires to see where he is, and where he was; that God has brought him from flesh to live in Spirit, from darkness, into the marvelous light; from the ways of sorrow, to that highway, the Lord Jesus.

And thus you see briefly, how, and in what manner, the soul beholds this mystical whore, the wisdom of the flesh. And so much shall suffice for the third question, namely, how the creature comes to attain to a sight of her?

We proceed now in order to the fourth question, which is, namely, When and how shall she be destroyed?

Now in brief to answer this, and so draw to a conclusion of the matter. I thus reply:

If then, O man! you desire to know how, and when this spiritual whore shall be destroyed: *it shall be done in the day, and by the coming and appearance of Jesus in you. This day is the last day; and this coming is the second coming of Jesus.* (Heb. 9:27–28)

Now as concerning this last day, know this, O Man! that it is nothing f or you to read the History of the last day in scripture, and there to see what shall be done in that day that *God will glorify Himself in the saints,* and be admired in all them that believe, that then God shall thoroughly purge His floor, *and the saints shall be like Him, for they shall see Him as He is.* Now, I say, it is nothing to know this in the History, except we know it in the Mystery of it.

You are therefore to expect Jesus to come to judgment in you: and the end of the world be in you. You are to wait for the return of this Jesus in Spirit; which shall come to you as He did to John, and show you the judgment of the great whore in you, f or there is nothing that shall happen or fall out to you in relation to the day of judgment, which shall not be verified in you in this life: though it may be, not in the same manifestative measure or fullness, as it shall be hereafter.

As first, one sign of this last day, is that there shall be wars and rumors of wars, nation shall rise against nation, and kingdom against kingdom. Now here Christian, you may behold the last day to be at hand, here is Gog and Magog at battle with the Lamb; what is it that makes all that envy, variance, strife, sedition, and emulation in the world: but the second, or spiritual appearance of Jesus in His people. The coming of Christ in the saints, is not to bring peace but a sword against us. I confidently say, that this last day, this spiritual appearance of Christ in men and women, is the very original of all these commotions that are amongst us; insomuch that now here is, the father hating the appearance of Christ in the son, the son likewise the father; the mother in the daughter, and the daughter in the mother, one brother sheathing the sword in the bowels of another, because the last day dawns, and the star of glory is risen more in one than in another. Here is Cain killing Abel, because his sacrifice is accepted of the Lord and the others is not. I tell you Christian, the more the whore will bestir herself, *she will not only raise outward but inward war against you: which inward insurrection and rebellion, is a symptom, that the day of judgment is at hand in you.* John tells us in Rev. 17:14 that "the kings of the earth shall make war against the Lamb," which kings in the Mystery, are but the kingly governing powers of your soul, which are assembled together in you, to this spiritual battle of Gog and Magog, to gage war against the innocent Lamb, Christ Jesus in spirit: but the Lamb shall overcome them, for he is King of kings and Lord of lords. All the power and policy of the flesh shall at last yield their power to Christ, and shall consent to the just judgment of the whore your fleshly wisdom. But till this strong man of the flesh be cast out, by that stronger than he, Christ Jesus, there will be nothing but war and confusion in you; so that indeed now the serpent is come down with great rage in you, knowing that he has but a short time. *The more nigh the coming of Christ is, the more this serpent spits out venom.* This Antichrist, this whore, will the more earnestly bestir herself, knowing it is but a short time to her judgment.

St. John tells us, Rev. 12:7, that when the woman had brought forth her manchild, which was to rule all nations with a rod of iron, the woman upon the birth of this manchild fled into the wilderness. And when the woman was in the wilderness, then says John, I saw war in heaven, Michael and his angels fought against the dragon, and the dragon fought and his angels (and what's all this to me?). Truly Christian, me thinks this war in heaven is a sure symptom of the day of the judgment, the end of this world in us, when God by His own power brought forth this man Jesus in us, and has given Him power to rule and reign in this woman, or weak passive Christian. The soul presently upon the birth or bringing forth of Jesus in it, is immediately in a wilderness, or lost in itself, and lies as one amazed at this sudden work of the Lord. In this bewildered condition of the creature, Satan he gages war upon it, shoots his fiery darts at it, pursues the woman with Herod, and seeks to devour both Christ and the Christian also.

Now therefore Christian, know that your soul is this heaven, where the great battle is fought. You being in a lost bewildered estate, as not knowing which way to escape the woundings of Satan, and the fiery darts of the wicked, but stand as a senseless, lifeless mark for your spiritual enemies to shoot at. But Michael your spiritual prince, Christ Jesus, He fights for you against the dragon, that whore, that Antichrist, that labors to devour you, so that you are the poor passive that lies stone still, while the serpent stings you, and the dragon exercises his cruelty upon you, till at last this Michael, our Prince Christ Jesus, has by His own power and strength, cast out, and so routed this dragon, this old serpent, vs. 9, that now his place is no more found in heaven or in your soul. Thus you may see Christ judging the whore, this serpent in you, insomuch, that now this loud voice is uttered from the heaven, or the soul of the saint, as in vs. 10: "Now is come salvation, and strength, and the kingdom of our God, and the power of his Christ." Whereas before, nothing but the dreadful voice of hell, wrath, anger, fury and judgment; nothing but wars and rumors of wars heard in your soul. *Yet now the day is come, Christ is come to judgment in us,* and has condemned the whore in us. *Now the voice of salvation is heard in you,* whereas before you apprehended God, as David did sometimes to have shot the arrows of his wrath at you, and to have battered your soul in pieces, by the thundering cannon of his wrath. Yet now you see there is a cessation of these tumults in you, and now you see that sweet messenger of God, the eternal Spirit, drawing near towards you with its white flag of peace, joy, comfort, and salvation, bringing comfort unto you by telling you your warfare is accomplished, your iniquity is pardoned, and you have received double at the Lord's hands for all your sins, (and then further) now strength is come also, which is another part of the voice of heaven, alas how feeble and how weak, faint, and unable was the soul before the spiritual resurrection of it? for the birth of this child Jesus in it, is the regeneration, or new birth of the Christian.

The wilderness the woman fled into is that mortified dead, lost estate of a Christian; the grave where the soul is buried to every living action. And the overcoming or conquering of the dragon, or the spiritual serpent, the wisdom of the flesh; is *the resurrection of a saint,* or that spiritual day of judgment of the whore in us. Now as Jesus raised up Himself by the power of the Father from out of the bowels of the earth, so by the strength and power of this Jesus, who is the resurrection and the life, a Christian rises out of this dead condition; and so her mortal putting on immortality, and corruption putting on incorruption, *here is death swallowed up in victory.* The Christian now as he has formerly been planted with Christ in the likeness of His death; so likewise now in the likeness of His resurrection. It bears now no longer the image of the first dead Adam, *but is risen in the likeness of Christ,* out of earth and flesh, which formerly he was involved and buried in, and by his rising again, overcomes the dragon by the blood of the Lamb, kills the great Goliath, the wisdom of the flesh, and this is all by the strength of the strongman Christ Jesus who is entered into this temple, or the heart of man, and silences all these earthly rumors and commotions in him; and also is the second part of the voice from heaven fulfilled, now is come not only salvation but strength.

And then thirdly, the Kingdom of God, that's come also, and the power of His Christ. Our Savior taught His disciples while He was in the flesh, and knew Him only after the flesh; I say, He taught them to pray, "Thy kingdom come," so that the kingdom of Christ, in that sense, was not yet come to the disciples. Even so it is with every poor Christian that has attained to no more knowledge than the flesh of Christ can teach them, that do not know Christ any other ways, than by the beholding of His fleshly substance, as Christians do in all outward and fleshly ordinances, that see no more or know no more of Christ, than bread, water and wine, and outward forms and order can teach them. The Kingdom of God is not come to them yet. While the woman was in the wilderness, the Kingdom of God was not come in her; but when she, by the strength of God was risen, and had overcome by the blood of the Lamb; then she cried, "now the kingdom of God is come." The woman was fed in the wilderness, vs. 6. In our low and lost estate, God feeds us with milk; because the kingdom of God, Christ in the measure of the Spirit, is not yet come to enable us to bear stronger meats. In the wilderness or weak condition of the saints, God feeds them with manna; but when He brings them into Canaan, He then compasses them about with the flowings of milk and honey.

This Canaan, is Christ, the true rest of a Christian, the kingdom of the Father in the saints, who draws up the soul from these low dispensations, by degrees, as it were, till he has seated it in Himself, into spiritual discoveries of His excellency; so that now the soul prays no more in the imbecility of the flesh, "Thy kingdom come," seeks no longer in fleshly forms and ordinances for the kingdom; for it is already in them, and they live in the enjoyment of it. Now is come salvation and strength, and the kingdom of God, and the power of His Christ. The dragon and his angels, they fought to establish their kingdom in the soul; but the Lamb overcame them, and set up His kingdom in the Christian; and the kings of the earth as namely, the powers of the creature bring all their glory and honor into it.

Thus you see that *the whore shall be destroyed, in the last day, at the second coming of Christ in us;* and likewise, I have discovered unto you one sign of the last day, or day of spiritual judgment; which is, those combats, wars, and commotions that are in a

Christian. I will but instance two more, and so shall draw to a conclusion.

Therefore secondly, a second sign or symptom of the last day, is the dissolution of the world; how that the earth, and all that is therein, shall be burned up; the sun turned into darkness, the moon into blood, the stars shall fall from heaven. And thus God will shake the heavens and the earth, and men's hearts shall fail them for fear; expecting the end of such sorrowful beginnings. Even thus it is with, and in a Christian, at the approaching of the Spirit of Christ in him: the world begins to be dissolved. The world is said to be placed in man's heart (Ec. 3:11); which world in man's heart, shall be dissolved by the fire of the Spirit of Christ. The heavens and the earth are mystically in man; and the waters, with their ebbings and flowings, are to be seen in the Mystery, in man. Here is God dividing the light from the darkness, to be seen in man; the waters below from the waters above the firmament. All this is fulfilled mysteriously in man; in whom God separates Himself, who is pure and light, from the darkness and nothingness of the creature. The fouls of the air, and fishes of the sea, are mystically in man; as namely, those flying fantasies, and swimming notions of the creature. In a word, here is everything bringing forth fruit after its own kind in man; and all God's creation, good in its own kind, in this first world, which is in manes heart.

But now this first world, this first creation, must be dissolved. Whatever excellency God has endued man with all, in this first creation; whatever maturity of wit and ingenuity the Lord has lent man; how high forever, and how large forever, the Lord has naturalized the creature, yet all this excellency shall vanish away. All this worldly glory, as I so call it, shall be consumed, and burned up. But alas! How hardly is this believed, how impossible is this to carnal man, that all this godly creation and work of God in his nature, should be annihilated; that reason, natural understanding, and wisdom; nay, nature itself, should be consumed. But this is the Lord's act, His strange act, His work, and wondrous work in a Christian.

Now therefore, consider Christian, that this is but the old-world, or first or lowest manifestation of God *in* you; which old-world must pass away and be no more. John tells us that he saw "A new heaven and a new earth," Rev. 21:1. "For the first heaven and the first earth was passed away, and there was no more sea." What's all this? Truly Christian in me it's this much: *when this day dawns, and this day star Christ Jesus arises in our hearts,* when the morning sun, even Jesus breaks forth upon us in His glory, warmth and splendor, *then begins this world within us to be dissolved.* The heavens and the earth in us, begins to meet with the fervent heat of the sun, and fall away to nothing. And the Lord instead of you, frames a new heaven and a new earth; so that all that was nature and pure reason, and ingenuity, is quite dissolved, and a new work wrought in the soul, that takes up the heart above its former excellency and glory. Although that were good in its kind, yet God will please, by the more glorious discoveries of Himself, to drown all this former creation, and to beget all things new in the creature; and then not only the heaven and the earth passed away, but also there was no more sea. This sea, or these waters in man, are these great over flowings, and inundations of nature; the swellings and roarings of proud self and creature. This deep silence shall be dried up by the heat of the Son of righteousness. These waters are the very throne of the whore, or the very seat of the wisdom of the flesh. Now when this sea shall be dried up, then there shall be a place no longer for this spiritual whore found in heaven, nor yet in the soul of a saint.

O, what a cause for joy is here for all the Saints! Yea, what eager pantings after the power and kingdom of Christ, should this beget and operate in us, to consider; that *in the day of Christ the whore shall be destroyed in us,* the sea shall be dried up and the heavens and the earth pass away.

If any man shall yet ask, when this last day shall come, and the end of the world accomplished? I answer then with Christ that "this generation shall not pass away, till all these things be fulfilled." All these things you must expect to be fulfilled in you, even in this life, O thou Christian, although happily not in the fullness and glory as shall be hereafter.

Tell me therefore, O thou experienced saint! Whose conscience can testify all these things to be true. How has the appearance of Christ in you, many a time confounded, as it were, all your natural vigor and power? How has it spoiled principalities and powers, the might and dominion of all natural excellency? How have you seen your self out of yourself as it were, above and beyond that earth you have been in formerly;

wrapped up with Paul, in the third heavens, as it were, beholding that glory, that all your old created light could never discern, living for a time in that peace which passes all understanding? Nay, shall I yet further tell you, at the second coming of Christ in us, our sun shall be turned into darkness, and our moon into blood. Our stars shall fall from their center; all that light from reason and nature; all those fleshly meteors, as also fixed stars, which have appeared at their several seasons in man, which did discover something of God to him. In a word, all the inferior with the superior discernings of God, that the creature has had formerly shall be extinguished, and shall appear to him to be but darkness and obscurity. The sun or the superlative light, shall be turned into darkness, and the moon, or that light which guides the more obscure part of man, shall be turned into blood, and confusion; and God will now create a new world in us. Old things shall pass away, and all things shall become new in us.

When the apostle spoke of the dissolution of the world, in 2 Pet. 3, he brings to mind the saints of the Mystery of that History, vs. 13. "Nevertheless we," says he, "according to his promise, look for new heavens and a new earth, wherein dwelleth righteousness." Although this old foundation and fabric shall be dissolved, and Christ that day of the Lord, shall come even as a thief in the night, and deprive us of all the excellency of our present station; waste, destroy, and burn up our gold, silver, and precious stones, consume all the glory of our present being, yet he speaks of one comfort, "we look for a new heaven, and a new earth, wherein dwelleth righteousness." *God never confounds the old, but He brings in a new.* The manner of God's new creation is to modelize the heart, to new mold the creature, to create a new Christian, as it were, to spiritualize the Christian. In a word, it is to swallow up the soul in Himself, to drown, confound, and bring to an end, all creature glory in His own incomprehensive excellency.

So that the saints are said to be that new Jerusalem that came down from God, decked and adorned with the glory of God only, as a bride adorned f or her husband. They are called new because *Christ in them has created a new-world.* This New Jerusalem had no temple in it of itself, but the Lord God and the Lamb were the temple of it. Truly that soul in whom the Lord God has made this desolation of creature excellency, and has created all things anew; this new Jerusalem, or new Christian, has no temple but Christ. In typical Jerusalem there was a temple, but Christ prophesied, that "There shall not be left here one stone upon another, that shall not be thrown down." (Mt. 24:2) Even so when God creates all things new in a Christian, He will demolish all that was in His stead, before He came to establish His new creation. Whatever the soul sees in any outward things, as forms, ordinances, worship, and the like, yet Christ will destroy and throw down, and bring to nought these things, and make Himself all this, and much more to a Christian. And thus you may see the day of judgment in a Christian. Here you may see Christ sending His Spirit into the worldly heart of man, convincing it of judgment, because the prince of this world is judged in him.

I proceed now to the third discovery of the last day, which is, namely, the destruction of Antichrist or the downfall of the whore; which does yet further manifest to us, that this last day in us; *the coming of this day of Jesus; and the appearance of this star in us, is the last day of the whore in us.* No sooner does Christ appear, but down falls the kingdom of the serpent, our fleshly wisdom. Therefore if you would know how this Antichrist shall be destroyed, the apostle tells us, 2 Thess. 2:8, that the Lord shall consume him with the breath of His mouth, and the brightness of His coming. This bright coming of Christ in us shall dispel that darkness and discover that fog that withholds or hinders the revelation of the whore.

Christ will then put aside this veil which is before this harlot's face; namely, all her specious pretenses, and shows of glory. Christ is that mountain spoken of in Is. 25:6, in whom God shall destroy the veil of the covering that is cast over all people. But this must be fulfilled, when this mountain, Christ Jesus, shall be established in the top of the mountain in our souls; or when Christ by His own power has seated Himself in us, above every high thought, and vain imagination. When the child Jesus is given to us, and has gotten the government upon His shoulders, this is the time of the whore's demolition in us. I say, it is the work of Christ by His coming in a saint, to discover the whore in him, to take away that veil of flesh, and those mists of obscurity, which this harlot has interposed between herself, and the soul.

When the day dawns, the darkness vanishes away. Even so, when this day of Christ Jesus dawns in your heart; when day breaks, as I may so say, in your soul, then begins the darkness in your heart to flee away, and now you come to be one of the children of the day. In a word, now you can see, discern and distinguish, and before you could not. Alas sirs! a poor soul that walks in darkness, and sees by no other light than the blaze of self, and by the sparks of his own f ire, he may be compared to a man who sees by candle light, who cannot discern one color from another. Even so it is with all natural men; they are not able to see what's good from evil, or what's light from darkness. O the palpable blindness of all poor creatures, in whom this day, Christ does not appear I This is to have eyes and see not, ears, and hear not.

This sad obscurity of a man that walks not in the light, may fitly be compared to that darkness which might be felt. The soul feels many times, what his blindness is, how it deprives him of the beautifical vision of God, brings him to wander from the way, Christ Jesus, causes him many times to stumble at that stumbling stone; and all this is, because the day is not dawned as yet. But now, *when the Son of righteousness arises in the soul,* why then, here comes light to them that sit in darkness, and in the shadow of death. Now this light guides the soul into the way of peace. It is said of New Jerusalem, Rev. 21, that it needed not the light of the sun, or of the moon, f or the glory of God did lighten it, and the Lamb was the light thereof, all which in me is this much: When God comes to create a new heaven and a new earth in a Christian, when He comes by the power of that regenerating Spirit, to make His Jerusalem a new Jerusalem, in this new estate, He will give her new light to walk by; so that now the saints shall have no need of the old sun, or the old moon; no need of the old light of reason, and nature, but here is new light brought forth now in the soul.

The new light is Christ, or the Lamb, who by radiant beams of His splendor, fills the soul with the glory of the Father, and destroys, or extinguishes all other inferior lights in the soul. We live in a generation wherein both Prefs (teachers, professors?) and Pulpit does cry down new lights, and truly I cannot much blame them that do so, because as yet they walk in the light of the old sun and moon, and are to be comprehended under the notion of the old Jerusalem. But tell me now? when the spirit of glory has darkened this sun and turned this moon into blood; quite confounded and brought to nothing the highest sphere of this natural excellency in them, when this old Jerusalem comes to be made new, then you shall hear a new voice crying up the new light of God manifested in them. O Christian! I tell you that you are a thrice happy man, to whom the Lord has made the Lamb the light. This Lamb-light is an innocent Light, a righteous Light, a pure Light, a discovering Light. It is this Light that discovers the hidden and obscure whore unto you. It is the Light of Christ that uncovers and strips the whore stark naked before you, of all her glory and excellency, so that now you behold her out of her purple and scarlet color, even in her very nakedness and shame. And thus you see how Christ in His day, in a Christian, does first of all discover the whore to him. But secondly, in this last day or sun rising of Christ in a Christian, it is the work of Christ to destroy, as well as to discover this whore in us, as it is the property of light to destroy darkness, so *it is the property of Christ to destroy Antichrist in the day of His appearance. It will be the work of Christ by His coming in you, to root out that spirit of Antichrist,* head and tail, root and branch, insomuch that there shall not be left one hoof of the beast in you. When John saw the angel come down from heaven endued with great power, Rev. 18, who enlightened the earth with his glory, immediately he heard this voice, "Babylon is fallen, is fallen, and is become the habitation of devils, the hold of every foul spirit, and a cage of every unclean and hateful bird," all which teaches me this much: that when that angel of the everlasting covenant, Christ Jesus, is by the Father sent down into the hearts of His saints, who comes by the power of His Spirit, and enlightens the earth or earthly man with His glory; when the earth is filled with the knowledge of the Lord; when the glory of the sun comes to enlighten and beautify our earthly hearts, this is the time of Babylon's downfall. Now is the season of the whore's destruction. *Now is the saint's time of Hallelujah.* Now rejoice over her thou heaven, and all the holy apostles and prophets, for God has avenged you on her, vs. 20. The prophet Malachi tells us, Chap. 4, that the day comes that shall burn like an oven. This day is Christ Jesus, who indeed shall so baptize us with the Holy Ghost, and Fire, as that He shall consume and burn up, waste and destroy all the appearances of the whore, the wisdom of the flesh. And therefore the same prophet tells us, chap. 3:3, that He shall sit as a refiner's fire, and as fuller's soap, and He shall purify the sons of Levi, that they may offer to the Lord, an offering in righteousness. This day must burn in us; this Jesus must be a refiner's fire to us, before we shall see the downfall of mystical Babylon. *The work that Christ has to do in us is to destroy mortality, and to clothe us with immortality; to destroy this corruption, and to clothe us with the incorruptible righteousness of Himself.*

After the downfall of the whore, Rev. 19, John tells us, vs. 8, that there was granted to the Lamb's wife that she should be arrayed in fine linen, clean and white. In this I observe, first, the love of Christ to the soul. Christ did first of all by His blood and passion, purchase the soul to Himself, to the end that she should be a constant spouse unto Him. But she has adulterized from her Husband; committed harlotry from her first Lover, and has taken part with Antichrist against Him; upon which adultery the jealousy of the Lord arises in Himself. And as jealousy is said to be the rage of a man, so the Lord, as I may say, in the rage of His jealousy, comes and destroys this Antichrist, stills sin in the Christian, sheaths the sword of the Spirit in the bowels of this spiritual Antichrist, breaks the head of this serpent in us; but yet notwithstanding, entertains this adulterized creature into His love and favor. You may see an emblem of His love in Hos. 3: 1, where God commands the prophet to go with a message of love to the woman who had played the harlot with him, "Go yet, love a woman beloved of her friend, yet an adulteress." Though she be an adulteress, yet I am her friend. Though she be an harlot, yet I send love greetings towards her. Though she has been inconstant towards me, yet I will own her to be my wife, my spouse, my beloved. And therefore the text says, that it was granted to the Lamb's wife that she should be arrayed in linen, clean and white, which likewise dictates to me:

In the second place, the purity that this day of burning, Christ Jesus in the Spirit, works in the heart of His people. He does not only take from it the garment spotted with the flesh, but likewise clothes it with the shining robe of righteousness. He does not only empty a soul of its own corruption, but likewise fills it with His glory, beautifies it with His own adornings. O fair, beautiful, amiable creature whose beauty and excellency consists in Christ, that divine center of brightness and glory. This will send a saint to the depth of admiration: "Behold, what manner of love the Father hath bestowed upon us, that we should be called the sons of God?" That God should thus by the power of His Spirit, consume all this dross and corruption in us, and bring us by that divine light to see our union with the Father, in the Son, and to see the glory of our adoption in Jesus and to behold ourselves in the flesh of our elder Brother at the right hand of the Father. *This is mercy past discerning and worth admiration.*

Thus will God, in the power of the Spirit, judge the spiritual whore in us; and cease us of the vassalage and servitude we were in to our own selves. Thus shall the brats of this spiritual Babylon, the wisdom of the flesh, be destroyed by that happy Man, Christ Jesus.

God says, Is. 13:12, concerning the destruction of Babylon, that He will "make a man more precious than fine gold, or the golden wedge of Opher. "This man is Christ, who in the day of His power and in the confounding of this spiritual Babel in us, shall be made unto us more precious than the highest creature excellency. *Never till now, will the saints come to value and to prize Christ, till they see what He does in them.*

Now, "how beautiful upon the mountains, are the feet of them that bring glad tidings of good things, that publisheth salvation, that saith unto Zion, thy God reigneth." Your messenger upon the mountains is Christ Jesus, who comes leaping over the mountains and skipping over the hills of difficulty that lies in the way, and appears in glory to His spouse or beloved Christian, and declares the message of glad tidings to him; namely, that his warfare is accomplished, that his iniquity is pardoned. The battle between Gog and Magog and the Lamb is finished, and the Lamb, or innocent Spirit, has overcome all by His power and strength; and now likewise He declares to Zion, or the soul of the saints that his God reigns. *Now is come the kingdom of our God, and the power of His Christ;* therefore *Hallelujah, for Babylon is fallen. The whore is destroyed* God has put it in the hearts of the kings of the earth (or powers of earthly man) to hate the whore, and reward her as she has rewarded them. And therefore again, *Hallelujah, for the Lord God omnipotent reigneth,* and the kingdoms of the whore are become the kingdoms of the Lord, and of His Christ.

All that remains behind therefore, is but one word of application, which shall be but only my exhortation to all poor souls that are groaning under this burdensome task and Egyptian bondage of the whore. Doubtless there are many to whom these my poor endeavors may offer themselves, whose portion is to groan under this spiritual vassalage, to labor under this body of death.

O Christian! whatever your condition be, cast not away your confidence, but wait upon the Lord and He shall renew your strength. *Expect the return or the second coming of Christ in you.* Pray daily that Christ's kingdom may come in you; that the Lord would establish His own throne in your heart. Expect *the* coming of *the* messenger of the covenant into His temple, or your heart, even the Lord Christ, whom you seek.

O! Labor to see that *Christ is approaching near you,* though the clouds of sin and wickedness hinder the sight of Him. Know also that this spiritual Son, Christ Jesus, will break away the clouds, will dispel the mists of iniquity in you, and will break out upon you, in His full warmth and splendor, and will bring you to walk in the light of His glory.

It was said of Abraham that he saw the day of Christ, and was glad. *How gladly then should the saints expect, and spiritually see this day to be at hand in them, in which they shall be freed from that burden which they now undergo?* Shall I tell you yet further, for your comfort, O Christian! This Jesus that comes, will come, and will not tarry. The Lord sees you in your poor weak condition. He takes notice of those many soils that your wicked heart gives you. He hears your sighings, cries and groans; He yearns after you; *He makes haste to come unto you so quickly,* as may contribute to the advancement of His glory, and your soul's further peace and comfort.

Thus in brief, I have discovered to you, in some measure, the Mystery of Iniquity, which works in all of us; the great whore, the spiritual Babylon, with her rise and her downfall.

In which poor treatise, I desire that those to whom it shall come, would thus understand me: that I do not by any wise seek hereby to set up my own opinion, as Antichrist, above others; but do only declare what I conceive from good reason, to be the manifestative mind of God unto me. And in all my mystical applying of any scriptures, I would not be thought hereby to endeavor the overture of the History; but only so much of the History as I see verified in me. In the Mystery, I have presumed in my present light, to declare to all men: what is of God. In my weak endeavors, I desire Him to make known, by the declarative power of His Spirit, what is of self. I desire to have a heart to disclaim it, when the Lord shall manifest it unto me. And so I commit my labor to Him, from whence only, I expect a reward; desiring nothing from any man, but a favorable construction of that which I have declared to all men, in the bowels of love and affection.

For my own part, I am one that waits for the kingdom and power of Christ to be manifested in me. I desire to see farther the glorious dawnings of Jesus, and risings of His glory in me; and *looking for, and hasting to the coming of the day of Jesus, in which all old things shall pass away, and all things shall become new.* And that which I conceive in this condition is the best course for myself to take, I shall likewise fasten the same advice upon all others.

"Who is among you that feareth the Lord, that obeyeth the voice of his servant, that walketh in darkness, and hath no light? Let him trust in the name of the Lord, and stay himself upon his God." (Is. 50:10)

December 12, 1647
Joseph Salmon

www.ingramcontent.com/pod-product-compliance
Lightning Source LLC
Chambersburg PA
CBHW021924040426
42448CB00008B/894